CAR TIPS FOR CLEAN AIR

". . . we continue to destroy even as we lament its
destruction."
—Jonathan F. King, Editor-in-Chief, *Sierra*

CAR TIPS FOR CLEAN AIR

HOW TO DRIVE AND MAINTAIN YOUR CAR TO CUT POLLUTION *AND* SAVE MONEY

ROBERT SIKORSKY

A PERIGEE BOOK

For Kyle, Mike, Jan and Jim, three new and one future driver, and all car owners everywhere, with hopes that we have the foresight to drive and maintain our vehicles in such a way to minimize their impact on the environment.

Perigee Books
are published by
The Putnam Publishing Group
200 Madison Avenue
New York, NY 10016

Material on the following pages first appeared in Robert Sikorsky's column "Drive It Forever" on the dates noted, and is used by permission of The New York Times Syndication Sales Corporation: pp. 7 and 8, April 4, 1987; pp. 22–24, Feb. 8, 1986; pp. 92–94, Nov. 2, 1985; and pp. 97–99, Jan. 10, 1987. The boxed material on pp. 19 and 20 is reprinted courtesy of Saab Cars USA, Inc. The material on pp. 52 and 53 first appeared in *Drive It Forever* by Robert Sikorsky, copyright © 1983 by Robert Sikorsky, published by McGraw-Hill, Inc.; reproduced with permission of McGraw-Hill, Inc.

Library of Congress Cataloging-in-Publication Data
Sikorsky, Robert.
Car tips for clean air: how to drive and maintain your car to cut pollution and save money / Robert Sikorsky.
p. cm.
ISBN 0-399-51649-2
1. Automobiles—Maintenance and repair. 2. Automobiles—Environmental aspects. I. Title.
TL152.S522   1991   90-44008 CIP
629.28'72—dc20

Printed in the United States of America

1 2 3 4 5 6 7 8 9 10

This book is printed on acid-free paper.

∞

CONTENTS

ACKNOWLEDGMENTS

The author would like to acknowledge the help of the following individuals, corporations and agencies that have contributed in some way to this book:

The New York Times Syndication Sales Corporation; Environmental Protection Agency (EPA); U.S. Department of Transportation (DOT); California Bureau of Automotive Repair (BAR); California South Coast Air Quality Management District; State of Arizona, Department of Motor Vehicles Emissions Testing; Washington State Department of Ecology; Robert Brooks, Technology Commercialization; Sam Leonard, General Motors Corporation; Ron De Fore, former U.S. Department of Transportation Deputy Assistant Secretary for Public Affairs and former Director of Public and Consumer Affairs at the National Highway Traffic Safety Administration (NHTSA); Motor Vehicle Manufacturers Association (MVMA); Clean Air Working Group (CAWG); American Petroleum Institute (API); The Business Roundtable; National Corn Growers Association; Renewable Fuels Foundation; Chevron U.S.A.; Allen Testproducts; Transportation Department, McDonnell Douglas Corporation; Hamilton Test Systems; *Automotive News*; Saab-Scania of America, Inc.; General Motors Corporation; Chrysler Motors; Ford Motor Company.

FOREWORD

YOU HOLD THE KEYS TO CLEAN AIR

Earth is a very forgiving and flexible planet. It's a lot like the big old cast-iron automobile engines of yesteryear. You could abuse them again and again, but because of their strong design, they had the capacity to recover and they kept running. But even those old behemoths, when taxed repeatedly, would finally give up the ghost. Earth could suffer the same fate if abuses against it don't stop. As grand a design as it is, the sphere is quite fragile and completely dependent on the interworkings of all its parts.

The abuses are the innumerable toxic wastes disgorged by man into the biosphere, and one of the biggest abusers is car exhaust. This seemingly inconsequential polluting by drivers, who don't understand or care that car exhaust can affect something so large, is a major ingredient of planet degradation.

The emissions from my car and your car, coupled with millions of others, can ultimately spell disaster. We don't need a nuclear war or a nuclear winter to ruin the planet. We can, and are, doing it with our cars, trucks and buses spewing millions of tons of toxins into the atmosphere. Unchecked, this poison will ultimately tax the recovery capabilities of Earth to such a degree that it will no longer be able to reverse the damage we inflict upon it.

Consider automotive maintenance and the role it plays in the preceding scenario. Every vehicle owner must realize that a vehicle carries with it an unwritten mandate to maintain it at its most efficient so as not to add more waste to the already overburdened atmosphere. *Indeed, maintenance, once the option of the car owner, should become a sacred responsibility.*

7

Each owner must make a commitment to maintenance but, unfortunately, many of us don't unless bold evidence of immediate rewards is placed smack-dab in front of us. We can be lazy and avoid responsible action until we see that taking care of a car is not only good for the car but essential for mankind and the planet we inhabit. In this book, I will show the benefits of environmental car maintenance—to you financially, to your car's performance and longevity, as well as to the Earth.

We *have* made admirable strides recently because some have cared about what is happening. Cars burn fuel more effectively, emissions have been greatly reduced, fuels are cleaner, oils more efficient. But these improvements are only as good as the owner's commitment to keep the car in the shape it was meant to be in.

Maintenance should never be avoided, even, for example, if you are selling your car in a year and know it can run that long without any care. Our main responsibility should be to ensure that our car is polluting as little as possible.

We need a whole new way of looking at automobile maintenance. We need to consider not only what the improvements will do for our pocketbooks, but what they will do for the environment, for Earth itself and, ultimately, for the health and well-being of all who live here. We each must take individual responsibility for our actions. The responsibility is not only to ourselves but to those who will come after us. Our generation is caretaker of the globe for only a brief period. Surely we can leave it in better condition than it is now.

In 1976 I dedicated my best-selling book *How to Get More Miles per Gallon* to my son, Kyle, with these words: "For my son Kyle, and all the children of his generation, with the hope that we may have the foresight to conserve fuel today so they may know the pleasure and responsibility of driving a car in the future." That was 15 years ago and the future is now: Kyle will be getting his driver's license in a few months. It is still my hope that he and his generation will know "the pleasure and responsibility of driving a car." But they must do it with a new sense of awareness and environmental concern.

—Bob Sikorsky
Tucson, Arizona

CHAPTER

1

A REMEDY FOR THE #1 CAUSE OF AIR POLLUTION

"None of our global environmental problems will be solved by industry alone. In the end, public values— translated into hard choices—will decide the future state of the planet."

—EDGAR WOOLARD,
Chairman of the Board,
DuPont Company

Motor vehicles are the number-one cause of air pollution in the United States. Each day cars, trucks and buses spew thousands of tons of pollutants into the atmosphere. Our motor vehicles account for a staggering two-thirds of the total carbon monoxide (CO) and about one half of the nitrogen oxides (NOx) and hydrocarbon (HC) emissions in the air. (See Figure 1 in Appendix.) Other noxious imprints cars leave in their wake are chlorofluorocarbons (CFC) and lead.

Carbon monoxide is a colorless, odorless and extremely poisonous gas. Its production is enhanced during engine idling and can even cause death to person in an enclosed garage.

Unburned or partially burned hydrocarbons are organic compounds such as paraffins, olefins, aromatics, aldehydes, keytones and carboxylic acids that contain hydrogen and carbon in varying amounts. A number of hydrocarbons are considered carcinogenic by health authorities. Nitrous oxides are poisonous gases that consist of colorless and odorless nitrogen oxide (NO) and the very toxic and odoriferous red-brown nitrogen dioxide (NO_2).

Chlorofluorocarbons, more commonly known as freon, are released by automobile air conditioners and contain fluorine, a poisonous gas that reacts with and depletes the earth's protective ozone layer, while lead—technically, tetraethyl lead—is an extremely toxic additive used in leaded gasoline to increase octane and provide valve wear protection.

Until recently carbon dioxide (CO_2), a major constituent of car exhaust, was thought to be harmless. Now it is being implicated as one of the main gases that contribute to global warming.

The environmental and economic impact of automotive pollution has been staggering: trees and other plants die, human health is adversely affected, the ozone layer is being depleted, increased carbon dioxide production contributes to the greenhouse effect—not to mention the heat generated by millions of engines and exhausts—and millions of consumer dollars are wasted each year.

We are fuel- and car-wasters. Our dependence on imported oil has never been greater. Our cars die before their time. Numerous studies, including a recent one by the AAA-Chicago Motor Club, have shown that owner negligence is the main reason most vehicles pollute needlessly. Add the fact that most people don't know how to drive environmentally and you have a one-two punch that is knocking out the environment. One need just look at the air in any major metropolitan area to know something is very wrong. Isn't it odd that you can now *see* "air"?

But we *have* made progress over the past two decades. Automotive emissions have been reduced significantly by the Clean Air Act. In 1970, "highway vehicle" emissions of Volatile Organic Compounds (VOCs) was 9.8 million metric tons. In 1987, it was 4.7 million metric tons. (VOCs are the unburned HC portions of gasoline.)

In 1970, automotive emissions of carbon monoxide (CO) totaled 64.2 million metric tons. By 1987, it had fallen to 33.4 million metric tons. Nitrogen oxides (NOx) emitted by highway vehicles, however, contributed the same or 33 percent of total

NOx emissions in 1987 as they did in 1970. Even though admirable progress has been made, motor vehicles still disgorge an abnormally high percentage of the pollutants found in our air. In 1987 highway vehicles contributed a whopping 54 percent of the total VOCs in the United States.

A plethora of books and articles about global warming, acid rain, pollution and the environment have poured out of newspapers and publishing houses. Curiously, nary a one has focused on the biggest source of pollution: the automobile. When it comes to the automobile's impact on the ecology, most car owners feel helpless or just don't care. They think there is nothing they can do, that the problem is too big—something for the government or the auto and oil industries to tackle. This attitude couldn't be more wrong. We *can* clean up the air; we *can* reduce automotive pollution. There are hundreds of things we can do with and to our vehicles to clean up the air and make our smog-infested cities healthier places to live. We *can* turn our vehicles into near-neutral environmental entities. This book will show you how.

The EPA reports that in 1987–89, 96 areas, mostly urban, failed to meet federal ozone standards; 41 areas violated the carbon monoxide (CO) standard. (See Appendix, Tables 1 and 2.) Urban smog reached record highs with the average maximum level of ozone 5 percent higher in 1988 than in 1983, the previous record year. U.S. emissions of carbon dioxide in 1988 were also the highest ever: 1.42 billion metric tons. Nearly 150 million Americans now live in areas that exceeded the federal maximum safe level for carbon monoxide or ozone pollution on at least one occasion during 1989. One health official characterized our nation's declining air quality as a "public health crisis."

While Congress wrestles with new provisions for the Clean Air Act, car owners can make a more positive environmental impact than all the acts Washington can conjure. While laws take years to implement, drivers can take *immediate* action. The singular beauty of "ecology driving" and "ecology maintenance" is that each of us can do something about cleaning up the air and the environment *right now, the very next time we drive a car.*

Ecology driving and maintenance is rooted in three basic facts:

—Drive your car efficiently and it will produce less carbon dioxide.

—Maintain your car properly and you will clean up auto-related emissions.

—Change your driving habits and you'll cut down on *all* harmful automobile emissions: CO, HC and NOx.

Anything you can do to lessen emissions will increase gas mileage and contribute to longer engine, transmission and axle life. Eco-driving and eco-maintenance can clean up the air, save you money, conserve energy, lessen our dependence on foreign oil sources, cut down on car repairs, increase fuel economy, extend car and tire life, and make us better and safer drivers. There is no real sacrifice involved. Once you learn to drive and maintain ecologically it becomes second nature. Everybody and everything wins: the car owner, the car, the environment.

No single consumer action will do more to clean the air and protect the environment than a commitment to drive and maintain our vehicles environmentally. Recycling aluminum cans, refusing or reusing polystyrene cups or sandwich containers, putting a brick in our toilet tanks, eliminating household hazardous wastes, planting trees, writing letters to editors are all admirable important steps, but nothing will do more for the air than environmental car care and driving. We can't put scrubbers on industries' smokestacks; we *can* in effect put scrubbers on our exhaust pipes.

I didn't write this book as an environmental panacea or as a sure and easy cure for a hundred years of humankind's misadventures. I did write it to offer to all drivers an anybody-can-do, economical and sensible, easy and effective method of driving and maintaining cars in a way that will immediately minimize their negative impact on the environment. The easy cost-effective methods herein will clean up car pollution if the suggestions are used "en masse." But remember, every little bit helps.

I have tried to hold technical material to a minimum; where it is used, I've explained it in everyday terms. The more of the book you incorporate into your daily driving and maintenance routines, the better.

2

ECO-MAINTENANCE: MAXIMUM CAR CARE FOR CLEAN AIR

"American automakers understand that industry, government and consumers must work together for a cleaner, more healthful environment. Cars are an essential part of the American way of life, and Americans are deeply committed to the integrity of the environment. We believe it is possible to have both, and we are willing to do our part."

—CHRYSLER MOTORS,
Ford Motor Company,
General Motors Corporation

Eco-maintenance is my concept of maintaining a car so that it operates as an environmentally neutral entity. Environmentally neutral means that the car operates with as little negative impact on the environment as possible. Eco-maintenance starts with the car owner, and you don't have to be a mechanic to practice it. Random inspections have shown that many cars are operating at partial efficiency and/or their emissions systems are suffering from neglect.

Only about 46 percent of all cars on the road today meet current tail pipe standards. These clean vehicles contribute only 16 percent of the total emitted hydrocarbons, 16 percent of the carbon monoxide, and 28 percent of the nitrogen oxide

13

emissions—when they are operating at maximum efficiency. So about half of all cars on the road produce more than ⅘ of the carbon monoxide and hydrocarbons and ¾ of the nitrogen oxide.

Pre-1983 cars account for 54 percent of all vehicles on the road today, but contribute a whopping 84 percent of all automotive hydrocarbon and carbon monoxide emissions and 72 percent of nitrous oxides. If you own an older car, keeping it in top condition is obviously a high priority. If you own a newer car, there are still many things you can do to lessen its emissions output.

A recent study by the Chicago AAA checked 558 cars that the owners volunteered for inspection and found a high degree of owner neglect. The study revealed that 55 percent of the cars tested had either low tire pressure, uneven tire wear or unsafe tread amount (usually less than 2/32 of an inch). In 37 percent of the cars the oil level was at least one quart low. Excessive emissions were found in 35 percent.

These are sorry numbers, but as numbing as they are they probably don't reflect the true state of automobiles on the road because the study was conducted with volunteered cars. No doubt the percentages would have been much higher were the cars chosen at random.

The emissions test done on the cars was conducted at low- and high-idle. Officials of the AAA-Chicago Motor Club say that many of the cars that passed would fail the federal road-load certification test, an emissions test conducted on cars under actual and not simulated driving conditions. They suggest the actual emissions failures may have been much higher.

General Motors notes in one of its car care ads that "industry experts estimate that half the cars and trucks on the road today are low on oil by a quart or more." If such a simple thing as correct oil level is neglected by so many drivers, just think of how neglected the rest of the car must be.

The *Chicago Tribune* (November 12, 1989) reported that a survey of 117 fleet administrators (the people who manage large fleets of cars for businesses) found that driver abuse (negligence) is "far and away the single most common reason for premature wear and breakdowns." Sixty-two percent of these managers "blamed breakdowns squarely on the drivers themselves."

When a car is new it is virtually pollution free, nearly a neutral environmental entity. But vehicle systems degrade because of owner negligence and improper driving techniques and is responsible for the majority of automotive emissions.

Air quality enemies: car owners who are meticulous about maintenance as long as their car is under warranty and they don't have to pay for it, but ignore the car once the warranty has expired and they have to pick up the tab.

We shouldn't tolerate that attitude anymore, in ourselves or others. We must all take full responsibility for our cars, driving and maintaining them at maximum efficiency at all times, not just when they are under warranty.

Motor vehicles can't maintain or drive themselves. They can't choose the type of fuel and lubricants they need. They can't control how often they are serviced. Car owners, however, can. We can fend off automotive senility and the accompanying symptoms of gasoline thirstiness, oil burning, and emissions proliferation. Here are a number of maintenance ideas to do so:

LOOK FOR LEAKS.

Try this the next time you park: Look at the parking lot surface. Unless it's a brand-new parking area, you'll see a cesspool of automobile lubricants and fluids compacted into unwieldy black, flat pancakes.

Talk about emissions! Talk about maintenance omissions! These pollution pancakes are prima facie evidence that we don't care for our cars. What we don't see are the millions of additional gallons that drip from our vehicles and evaporate into the air.

The escaping fluids cause other problems. They lie hidden in the pores and spores of our roads until reactivated by rain.

Then they pop to the surface and cover the roads with a fine slippery coating that makes driving hazardous.

To counter the pancake revolution, do a simple driveway inspection each day. Glance at the spot where you park your car. Drippings and droppings are visual red flags. It's easy to "spot" leaks and have them fixed before they become costly problems. Ideally, all environmentally maintained cars should be tight, leak-free "sealed" units.

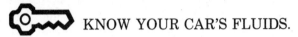 KNOW YOUR CAR'S FLUIDS.

Brake fluid, transmission fluid, motor oil, radiator antifreeze/coolant, gasoline, power steering fluid, windshield wiper solvent, these are the fluids to watch for. Learn what the various colors indicate, and notice from what area of the car they are dripping—front, middle or rear.

Color	Fluid
black or dark brown	motor oil or grease
yellow or green	coolant or antifreeze
pink or red	transmission fluid
clear	brake fluid, power steering fluid, or unleaded gasoline

The only harmless fluid is the water that collects when condensation drips from the air conditioner after use.

 DETECT FUMES.

Gasoline usually signals its presence to your nose before your eyes. Because they are the most harmful to the air, gasoline leaks should be repaired at once.

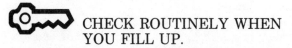 CHECK YOUR TAIL PIPE.

Want a clue to your engine's health? After it has cooled, walk to the back of your car and look at the inside of your exhaust pipe. Rub your finger around the inside. The color and condition of the deposit are indicators of engine condition. The engine leaves its imprint on the tail pipe much like your heart, via an EKG, leaves its imprint on a sheet of paper.

If the deposit is wet, black, sooty or smells of gasoline, the carburetor may be set too rich or the automatic choke needs adjustment or the engine needs tuning. If the deposit is oily and black, it could indicate worn piston rings or valve problems. A black tail pipe is a sure sign the car is blackening the air outside.

If the deposit looks white and glazed, the engine may be running too hot, the timing is incorrect or there may be an intake manifold leak, all conditions that increase pollution.

Ideally, the tail pipe should be coated with a powdery light gray-brown fluff. If yours is any other color, something isn't right with the engine or the emissions controls or catalytic converter.

TRUST YOUR SENSES.

Use your senses all of the time. Sight, smell, sound and feel can tell you much about your car. Anytime you smell something unusual or see a leak or hear a noise or feel a vibration, you know something is amiss. Have your car checked as soon as possible to limit possible damage.

CHECK ROUTINELY WHEN
YOU FILL UP.

With the burgeoning popularity of self-serve gasoline stations, today's owners tend to ignore their cars more than in the past. If you use self-serve, be sure to check your oil and tires and coolant and other fluids each time you get gas. Also, do the additional environmental inspections and services suggested in this book. Jumping out of the car and pumping gas, overlooking simple maintenance checks and services, may be the number-one reason so many cars are woefully out of trim.

 KEEP TIRES FIRM, NOT FLABBY.

Adding air to the inside of your tires is one of the kindest things you can do for the air outside them. I doubt if there is any easier maintenance practice. Proper inflation is a key to long tire life and helps the vehicle last longer because the engine doesn't work as hard to move the car. Firm tires mean more miles per gallon, and that equates to a reduction in vehicle exhaust pollution. They are also much safer than flabby ones.

No single owner practice will yield so many benefits for so little time invested—and at no cost! Air is free, and anyone can learn to put it in their tires. I suggest inflating tires to the *tire manufacturer's* recommended maximum pressure printed on the sidewall of the tire, usually between 32 psi (pounds per square inch) and 36 psi. If you don't know how to check tire pressure and fill tires, ask a service station attendant to show you. Tire pressure should be checked at least every two weeks at a time when the tires are cool.

 SERVICE YOUR AIR CONDITIONER.

According to the California Department of Consumer Affairs, leaky car air conditioners are the single greatest source of chlorofluorocarbons (CFCs), a very active greenhouse gas more commonly known as freon. Finding air conditioner leaks is a job for the professionals.

The air conditioning system should be tight and leak-free, and the best way to guard against air conditioner leaks is to have the unit thoroughly serviced each year.

 CHOOSE AN ECO-CONSCIOUS
A/C SERVICE

When you have the air conditioner serviced at a professional repair shop, inquire first if they use chlorofluorocarbon recovery equipment. Most shop owners know suppliers who carry this type of A/C equipment. It usually says something like "Environmentally safe CFC (freon) recovery used here." Look for shops that advertise this. The old practice was to release the evacuated freon directly into the atmosphere. Up to now, technicians had no idea that freon was contributing to the destruction of the atmosphere's protective ozone layer.

The ozone layer, as you probably know, shields the earth against the strong rays of the sun. Its thinning could have a dramatic effect on the way we live, the crops we grow, the weather—the entire ecosystem.

 KEEP A/C SEALS PLIABLE.

A trick you can use to keep the freon inside where it belongs is to run the A/C occasionally during the cold months, which helps to keep the various seals pliable. Supple seals contain better; ignored air conditioner seals allow freon to escape. This simple trick will do a lot for your A/C and for the ozone layer.

MONTREAL PROTOCOL

The ozone depletion controversy recently led to the signing of the Montreal Protocol, an agreement by many of the world's nations to limit and phase out the use of CFCs and the use of R-12 (freon) by the year 2005. But we can start phasing it out right now.

"A new, environmentally safe air conditioning refrigerant will begin to replace the current R-12 fluid—commonly referred to as freon—in Saab passenger cars during 1991," says the carmaker.

"The new fluid is a chlorine-free refrigerant known as HFC-134a and is not in the chlorofluorocarbon (CFC) family. CFCs have been found to have a detrimental effect on the earth's ozone layer, which serves to protect the environment from the sun's ultraviolet rays, and have been considered to be a possible factor in global

warming. . . . Sweden has . . . drawn upon its own reduction plan to accelerate, its phase-down (in use of
CFCs) by 1995, and in the United States, Vermont has
restricted the use of R–12 in new car air conditioners
from 1993.

"The air conditioners which are installed in Saab 9000
and 900 models are presently being re-engineered to accept HFC–134a, and to take full advantage of its environmentally safe properties. The cooling capacity and
performance of these systems will not be influenced. . . ."

STAY TUNED.

One of our most important obligations is to have our vehicles
tuned regularly. It's especially crucial during winter months
when emissions are higher and dense outside air tends to
create situations that seal in the bad air over our cities. A
properly tuned car ensures emissions are being held to a minimum.

Each time a plug misfires, there is a consequent increase in
emissions. One spark plug in a V–8 engine misfiring only half
the time at 55 mph will also reduce gas mileage by a full 7
percent. Two plugs misfiring at the same speed cuts mileage not
by twice the amount of one plug misfiring, but nearly triple, or
20 percent. Those numbers become even more impressive in
smaller engines.

Dirty carburetors or fuel injectors, clogged air filters, worn
points and plugs, and an ignored ignition system not only waste
gas and lower engine performance, they cause increased emissions of particulate matter and nitrogen oxides, two of our most
persistent smog problems. Any "complete" tune-up should include a thorough examination (and repair, if necessary) of the
exhaust emissions *and* evaporative control emissions systems.
(See Chapter 3.) An "environmental" tune-up should also include a diagnostic check of the engine's sensors and on-board
computer.

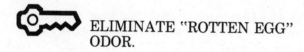

CHECK YOUR CHOKE.

Have you ever seen a car with gasoline dripping out of its tail pipe? One of the major atmospheric violators is a too-rich automatic choke. It's a pollution gremlin's delight. Ignore the choke and you'll have raw gasoline coming out the tail pipe and unburned hydrocarbons coming out your ears.

Correct automatic choke operation is vital for fast cold-starts. If the choke is set too lean, it won't permit enough gasoline into the engine and the car labors to start; if too rich, it floods the engine with extra gasoline, again causing a hard-start condition. The over-rich setting forces the choke to stay closed longer, and this causes the engine to run rich, even when it is warm. A choke that doesn't open fully and quickly is murder on emissions. Choke adjustment is an easy job for any mechanic.

ELIMINATE "ROTTEN EGG" ODOR.

Many new-car owners have complained about "rotten egg" odor, which comes from sulfur in the gasoline. After gasoline is burned and the exhaust moves into the catalytic converter, it undergoes a chemical reaction. The converter "converts" the sulfur to hydrogen sulfide (H_2S), a gas most of us remember well from high school chemistry class. The more oxygen available to the converter during this process, the stronger the smell. Any raw gasoline that comes in contact with the hot converter intensifies the odor.

To say the least, hydrogen sulfide doesn't smell very good and doesn't do our air any favors. Here are some methods that will keep rotten eggs out of your car:

—Try different brands of gasoline. One may have less sulfur than another.
—Use an emissions-control system cleaner, available at gasoline stations and auto-supply stores.
—Check engine timing for proper setting.

—Ask a technician if altering the fuel/air mixture or recalibrating the engine computer will help.

—Lay off the full throttle accelerations; they create more emissions. They also intensify rotten egg odor.

 AVOID PLUGGED PLUGS.

If you drive a lot in the city, consider changing to spark plugs *one* heat range higher. Slow stop-and-go tends to foul plugs, cause engine miss and create more pollution. A higher heat range plug burns hotter and isn't as likely to gunk up. Check with your mechanic to see if hotter plugs can safely be installed on your car.

 "RISING" TO THE OCCASION.

On older cars the heat riser or manifold heat control valve helps speed engine warm-up. This thermostatic valve closes off a portion of the exhaust manifold when the engine is cold, forcing hot exhaust gases to one side of the manifold. As the engine warms, the valve opens and routes the exhaust gases to both sides.

Technically, this valve isn't considered an emissions control device, but in actuality, it is. If it is stuck open, the engine takes longer to warm and creates a lot of unnecessary pollution. If stuck closed, the engine may overheat. The heat riser should receive regular service—usually a few drops of solvent is all it needs. A good tune-up includes servicing of this very important component.

 DON'T BURN OIL.

If your car is burning oil—blue or white-blue smoke coming out of the tail pipe—it is creating pollution. Oil burning doesn't always mean that the entire engine needs rebuilding, the cure may be much less expensive and could be as simple as changing brands of oil.

READ YOUR OWNER'S MANUAL.

It's chock-full of information you need to drive and maintain your car correctly. From oil change intervals to driving techniques, from cold-start methods to emissions system servicing intervals, the owner's manual is indispensable. Read it, understand it and follow its advice. If you don't have an owner's manual you can order one from the company listed in the Resource Guide.

DON'T DUCT THIS ISSUE.

Does your car exhibit any of the following symptoms: poor starting, loss of power, rough running, excessive emissions? And you say you had a tune-up not too long ago? And your gas mileage has dropped too?

Before you give the beast two aspirin, cross your fingers and send it to bed, perhaps you should check one of the most ignored under-the-hood items. In fact, these parts feel so neglected that they go to bed many evenings with tears coming out of their ducts.

Oops! Gave it away. Yep, I'm talking about the carburetor and fuel-injection air ducts. Air ducts come in many sizes and shapes, but they all perform the same function. They route air to your car's engine.

There are two types of air ducts: fresh-air inlet ducts and preheater ducts. Fresh-air ducts supply outside air to the engine when it is warm, and preheater ducts supply preheated air to the engine during the cold-start and cold-engine warm-ups and operation.

Just as all roads once led to Rome, all air ducts lead to the engine air cleaner. The fresh-air duct provides air from some point near the front grill, and preheater ducts get warm air from some point on the intake manifold of the engine.

Both types of ducts look like overgrown hoses that have a corrugated, crinkly skin. The fresh-air duct is usually made of some type of fibrous material, and the preheater duct is typically fabric-covered aluminum. If these ducts are missing, have loose connections or have been damaged by punctures or by being squeezed shut, they could be causing your engine's poor performance.

The amount and temperature of the air fed to an engine is of extreme importance to its performance, economy and durability. If a fresh-air duct is missing or damaged, the engine must rely on under-the-hood air to keep it going. Most engines don't like that, especially if it is a hot day, and the resultant fuel and hot air mixture causes it to perform erratically.

The same is true of the preheater duct. If it is damaged in any way, the engine can't receive correct amounts of preheated air under cold operating conditions. Without preheated air, the engine gets confused, cantankerous. It doesn't like running on cold air when it, too, is cold. It needs its fix of preheated air when it is warming up, and the preheater duct provides it. Once the engine has warmed to the correct operating temperature, a thermostatically controlled valve in the air cleaner closes. This shuts off the supply of preheated air and allows fresh air to enter by way of the fresh-air duct.

Many pre-1975 cars do not have carburetor air ducts. Look for special openings on your air cleaner to determine if it is one that should be fitted with ducts.

Take a few minutes and check those air ducts on your engine. If loose, they should be tightened; if damaged, they should be replaced; if absent, new ones should be installed. Give your engine what it craves—hot air when it is cold and cool air when it is hot. It will repay you with more miles per gallon, better performance, reduced emissions, easier starting, less stalling and no carburetor icing.

Air ducts are easy to replace and relatively inexpensive. They can be found at most auto-parts stores.

 USE A CLEAN AIR FILTER.

The air filter cleans the air the engine uses. A dirty air filter forces the engine to use more gasoline. This causes unnecessary pollution. Air filters should be changed according to the manufacturer's suggestions. If you drive in dusty areas or on dirt roads, change the filter more often.

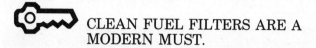

CLEAN FUEL FILTERS ARE A MODERN MUST.

Fuel-injected cars require clean fuel filters because they are more discriminating about a gasoline's cleanliness. Clogged or dirty fuel filters on injected cars are a main cause of poor performance. Be certain yours is changed—whether you own a carbureted or fuel-injected car—at least as often as the manufacturer's maintenance schedule prescribes, more often if you drive under dirty or dusty conditions or have been forced to use inferior-quality fuel. (For fuel-injector maintenance see Chapters 5 and 6.)

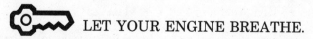

NEVER SWITCH TO A COOLER THERMOSTAT.

Newer cars use high-temperature cooling system thermostats so they can run hotter. Don't change to a lower one. Newer engines are designed to run hot. Heat increases efficiency and reduces emissions. A cooler thermostat will create problems and pollution. If you bought your present car used, check to see it has the correct temperature thermostat. The previous owner could have switched it.

Make sure the thermostat is operating properly. If it isn't opening or closing on cue, the engine will run inefficiently. Keep an eye on your temperature gauge. If the engine takes a long time to warm to normal operating temperature, or if the gauge always seems to be in the marginally hot area, have the thermostat checked for proper operation.

LET YOUR ENGINE BREATHE.

If your engine has a breather cap on the valve cover (it's usually the place where you add oil), it should be clean and free of obstructions. The breather cap should be cleaned and serviced regularly. It allows the engine's crankcase to "breathe" in fresh air, which dilutes pollution-laden crankcase fumes and makes them easier to burn.

Place your hand near the breather cap and see if you can feel any air coming out. If you do, that's a sure sign the engine needs attention. The breather cap is supposed to draw fresh air into the crankcase system. If, instead, air is coming out—a condition known as blowby—heavy doses of hydrocarbons will escape into the air. Because the hydrocarbon content of crankcase gases can be much higher than that of the exhaust, this condition should be corrected fast. Unfortunately, escaping blowby gases are a much too common and ignored phenomenon of older vehicles.

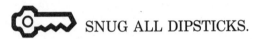 SNUG ALL DIPSTICKS.

Be certain that the oil, transmission and other dipsticks are pushed down tight. This keeps fumes from escaping from the openings.

 STORE IT DRY.

If you are going to store a vehicle for a long time, drain the fuel tank and carburetor and gas lines. Otherwise the fuel in these systems, especially if they are older "open" systems, will eventually evaporate. (And while you are at it, check those gas cans in your garage to see that the caps are securely fastened and the vent holes closed. Power lawn mower users, be certain to drain your mower at the end of the season and put it away dry.)

 REPAIR FAULTY EXHAUST.

If the exhaust system is loose or has holes in it—especially that portion between the catalytic converter and the engine—untreated pollutants can vent directly into the air.

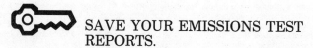

ENGINE BACKFIRE.

Don't treat a backfiring engine lightly. Peugeot recently noted that four consecutive misfires can totally destroy a catalytic converter. A misfiring or backfiring engine should be investigated immediately.

OIL CHANGE AND OIL QUALITY.

In Chapter 6 the merits of using an Energy Conserving II oil are discussed. Frequent oil changes, preferably with this type of oil, are a must. Follow the "severe service" oil change interval recommended in your owner's manual or change oil and filter at least every 3,000 miles or three months, whichever comes first. Ideally, the interval should be shortened in the winter.

Use a high-quality API SG-rated oil. There is some evidence that a lower-quality engine oil can deposit on the catalyst in the catalytic converter, reducing its efficiency.

SAVE YOUR EMISSIONS TEST REPORTS.

Save your emissions test reports. Years ago I bought a 1975-model car that had over 100,000 miles on it. I had no idea of how it had been treated but wanted to find out how far it could go without a major repair.

I took the vehicle in for emissions testing and it passed with readings of 29 parts per million (ppm) hydrocarbons (allowable limit is 250 ppm) and 0.53 percent carbon monoxide (allowable limit is 2.2 percent).

A year and 35,000 miles later, the car's readings had dropped to 21 ppm HC and 0.16 percent CO. After another 32,000 miles it showed further drops in both emissions. Hydrocarbons were cut in half to 11 ppm, while carbon monoxide dropped to 0.13 percent.

My point is this: the reports showed me that I was doing

something right, because the car continued to improve with age instead of deteriorating as most older cars do. The reports verified that a careful plan of preventive maintenance was paying real dividends: the car got better mileage, produced fewer emissions and is still running strong today with only token environmental impact.

If I can do it with my older car, there is no reason you can't do it with yours. Emissions reports are both clues and helping hands in your quest for non-impact driving.

State emissions testing facilities, in essence, take a "slice" of the exhaust and read the CO, HC and NOx content in relation to the total volume of the slice. The amount of toxic emissions are then listed in either percentages or parts per million (ppm). For instance, a reading of 1.52 percent carbon monoxide means

STATE OF ARIZONA   D 0623094

VEHICLE INSPECTION REPORT
CERTIFICATE AT BOTTOM NEEDED FOR REGISTRATION

Thank you for helping clean up our air. Your vehicle's test results are shown below. If it passed, tear off the certificate and submit it with your registration documents. If your vehicle failed its first inspection, it must be repaired and retested before it can be registered. To qualify for a free retest, the vehicle *must be returned within 60 days, accompanied by this report properly signed and certified on the reverse.* **Note:** Repairs may be covered by the 5 year/50,000 mile warranty provisions of the Clean Air Act. Check your owner's manual or contact your auto dealer for details.

Registration Deadlines: Failed vehicles are not subject to a late registration penalty *as long as* the first inspection was performed before expiration of registration and the registration renewal is received by the auto license department within 30 days of the first test.

EMISSIONS INSPECTION			EQUIPMENT INSPECTION				FINAL RESULT
Cruise	Idle	Opacity	Air System	Fuel Inlet Restrictor	Presence of Lead in Fuel	Catalytic Converter	
-----	PASS	-----	PASS	PASS	PASS	PASS	PASS

VEHICLE INFORMATION

License Plate	Plate Code	Vehicle Identification No.	Year	Make	Style	Fuel	Mileage
BHT401---	---	VC24415B1066484----	75	VOLVO	4DSD	G	000,000

EXHAUST EMISSIONS READINGS
(Cruise Readings for 1980 & Older Vehicles Are for Diagnostic Purposes Only)

	INITIAL IDLE (1980 & Older Vehicles)		CRUISE			FINAL IDLE	
	HC (ppm)	CO(%)	HC (ppm)	CO(%)	Opacity (%)	HC (ppm)	CO(%)
Maximum Allowable	00250	02.20	-----	-----	-----	-----	-----
Vehicle Readings	00028P	00.12F	-----	-----	-----	-----	-----

that 1.52 percent of all exhaust coming from the car consists of carbon monoxide. A reading of 200 ppm HC, on the other hand, is another way of expressing a percentage. Just divide 200 by 1,000,000 to get 0.02 percent. However, testing stations use ppm instead of percentages whenever amounts are small.

Government emissions tests are conducted over measured road courses and not stationary testing, as in state facilities. The emissions production of cars tested is therefore measured in grams per mile (gpm).

Current California emissions standards limit vehicles to .39 grams per mile (gpm) HC; 7.0 gpm CO and .7 gpm NOx. Current federal standards are .41 HC; 3.4 CO and 1.0 NOx. These standards apply for 5 years or 50,000 miles to all vehicles currently in use.

As of May 1993, California will tighten its standards to .25 gpm HC; 3.4 gpm CO and .4 gpm NOx. The current administration-proposed standards are nearly identical to the 1993 California standards, differing only in the amount of NOx: the federal limit being 0.7 gpm. The tougher California standards will apply for a longer time too—75,000 miles for in-use vehicles.

You should note that different states use different measuring methods, with units of either parts per million (ppm) or grams per mile (gpm). Find out about the methods and limits in your state.

If you live in a state that doesn't require emissions testing, you can still use these standards as yardsticks by which to measure your car's pollution performance. By adhering to these strict standards, you will contribute to clean air.

 LOG IT.

Keep a detailed log of any and all car maintenance: what service was performed, when, and at what cost; how many miles per gallon on each fill-up; emissions test results; next scheduled maintenance and so on. You'll have a handy record to fall back on and a future list of things to be done to keep the car from deteriorating.

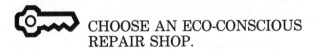 **CHOOSE AN ECO-CONSCIOUS REPAIR SHOP.**

It's in the quality repair and service facilities of this nation that consumers will find their best defense in the battle against vehicular pollution. At no time since the car was invented has the technician's role been more important.

An incompetent or untrained mechanic can wreak havoc with a modern engine, turning it into a polluting monster. It has never been more imperative for consumers to find a competent repair shop, one that has the customer's—and society's—best interests at heart. A shop that will keep your car in proper tune, will service it when it should be serviced and will practice preventive maintenance is essential to keeping vehicular emissions at a minimum.

BE AN ECO-WATCHER.

Eco-maintenance means watching other cars besides yours. In California, residents can call a toll-free number (1-800-CUT-SMOG) to report cars, buses and trucks that emit visible smoke exhaust for more than 10 seconds. Drivers of these polluters are then advised in writing by the state to make repairs. Currently, about 8,000 vehicles each month are reported.

Although all states don't have pollution hot lines—and all states should!—you can still report the license numbers of visibly polluting vehicles to the air quality management board or health department of your city, county or state government.

3

THE HEART OF ECO-MAINTENANCE: CARING FOR THE EMISSIONS CONTROL SYSTEM

Tail pipe emissions (exhaust gases) are the by-products of the "incomplete" combustion of gasoline and air. If an engine could burn 100 percent of the gasoline, the only "emissions" produced would be water, carbon dioxide (CO_2) and heat. But that's not the case. (See Figure 2 in Appendix.) Gasoline and air aren't "pure," and an engine operates only at 20- to 30-percent efficiency. It wastes 70 to 80 percent of the energy in a gallon of gasoline.

When a vehicle burns 100 gallons of gasoline, it produces 90 to 120 gallons of water and 3 to 10 gallons of unburned fuel. The actual quantities are determined by how much throttle you apply to accelerate and how efficiently your engine is operating. You also produce ½ to 2 pounds of sludge and ¼ to 1 pound of resins and varnishes, which not only settle to the bottom but collect on valve stems and pistons. The combustion process produces 1 to 5 pounds of nitrogen and sulfuric acids and 6 to 10 ounces of insoluble lead salts (if leaded gasoline is burned). In addition, huge quantities of carbon dioxide (CO_2), toxic carbon monoxide (CO), unburned hydrocarbons (HC) and nitrogen oxides (NOx) are generated.

To top it all off, sunlight adds its finishing touch, reacting with exhaust gases to form peroxides, ozone and peroxyacetyl-nitrates—the main constituents of smog.

You can call it exhaust, pollution, emissions or smog: whatever the name, one look at the above leaves little doubt that tail pipe fluff isn't good for anything.

There are two general categories of automotive emissions. The first is the one we are most familiar with, the exhaust emissions that come from burning gasoline. Lesser known are the evaporative emissions. These are the hydrocarbons (HC) released into the air when gasoline evaporates. A third unacknowledged group are emissions contributed by fluids that leak from the car: Radiator coolant, motor oil, brake fluid, power steering fluid and transmission fluid all leave their marks on the air, not to mention on our roads and driveways.

 UNDERSTAND YOUR EXHAUST
EMISSIONS CONTROL SYSTEM.

All vehicles built after 1975 have some type of emissions control system. You should be familiar with yours and know where the various parts or sensors are located and what they do. It's not as hard as it seems.

At first glance the underhood paraphernalia is enough to scare even a seasoned technician, but having someone with knowledge explain to you what to look for can make the maze amazingly simple. Once you know where to look, visual inspection is easy: Are all the wires connected; are there any loose hoses or vacuum lines; is the filter dirty; are the belts tight and not worn? Emissions parts can be checked each time the car is serviced or whenever the hood is opened.

MAKING SENSE OF SENSORS

There are a number of electronic and mechanical devices on your engine that make up the emissions control system. If any one of these becomes defective, harmful tail pipe emissions will increase. It's important that *all* emissions controls work *all* the time. A car may be able to run rough even if one or two sensors aren't working, but it will pollute to the high heavens. Let's review the role some of these devices play in keeping car exhaust clean.

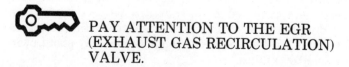 CHECK YOUR OXYGEN (O_2) SENSOR.

The oxygen sensor is placed in the exhaust stream and, as its name implies, reads the oxygen content in the exhaust gases. This information is relayed to the engine's computer, which then adjusts the fuel/air mixture for top efficiency and minimal emissions.

Recently the Environmental Protection Agency reported that the failure of the oxygen sensor dramatically increased the emissions of unburned hydrocarbons (HC) and carbon monoxide (CO). In a test with a faulty O_2 sensor, unburned hydrocarbons emissions skyrocketed to 445 percent above normal while carbon monoxide emissions increased by 1,242 percent. Obviously, driving around with a bad O_2 sensor is not environmentally sound.

Another study, conducted for the EPA by the Radian Corporation, found that the O_2 sensors are the most trouble-prone of all emissions system parts. It noted that in a group of fuel-injected cars that failed the California emissions test, 68 percent of the failed vehicles needed a new O_2 sensor.

Different car manufacturers have different servicing and replacement schedules for O_2 sensors. As you can see, it is imperative that yours is checked with every tune-up and at the recommended service intervals.

PAY ATTENTION TO THE EGR (EXHAUST GAS RECIRCULATION) VALVE.

EGR systems control nitrogen oxides (NOx) emissions by keeping engine combustion temperatures below that which produces NOx. If the EGR senses the engine temperature getting too high, it reroutes a small amount of the exhaust to mix with the incoming air/fuel. This dilutes the fuel charge and lowers combustion temperatures and reduces nitrogen oxides.

Most cars have an EGR service light that glows when this important valve needs attention. I've seen drivers disconnect this light because they don't want to be bothered. The light serves an important environmental function. Drivers should heed it.

 CHECK YOUR PCV (POSITIVE CRANKCASE VENTILATION) VALVE.

On some older cars the PCV valve *is* the entire pollution control system. It's a simple check valve—it allows unburned gases to flow one way but not the other—that meters unburned combustion products back into the engine to be reburned. The PCV valve is normally located on the valve cover or on the side of the engine block. If it is inoperative or dirty, the unburned fuel will be routed directly into the atmosphere instead of being reburned.

PCV valves are not costly, are universally available and are easy to replace. Most give years of trouble-free life. To check the valve yourself, simply pull it out of its housing and shake it. It should rattle freely. If the valve is stuck or dirty, change it rather than clean it. They are quite inexpensive.

Some PCV systems have disposable filters located inside the air cleaner that should be replaced when dirty. Filters made of wire mesh can be cleaned, reoiled and replaced.

Here's a product I recently came across and am using on my vehicles. It's called the "Auto Economizer" and is an elegantly contrived and patented filter that can be used in all cars equipped with a PCV system. It inserts into the line where the PCV valve is located and needs replacement only about every 30,000 to 40,000 miles.

The Auto Economizer filters out large particulates, sulfur, carbon, varnish, acids, resins and high-molecular-weight materials before they are reintroduced into the engine via the PCV system. It also contains a water-condensing grid that collects water vapor from the crankcase and keeps it in a separate compartment. A limited amount of this condensate is then injected into the engine upon restart.

By filtering out these impurities before they are drawn into the combustion chamber the engine is fed clean, instead of contaminant-laden, air. The results, according to the maker, are a cleaner engine and spark plugs, extended oil, oil filter and spark plug life, a more efficient engine, enhanced fuel economy, extended life of emissions control components, especially the catalytic converter, and reduced noxious emissions into the environment.

At present the Economizer is available only by mail. For more information write: The Mileage Company, Box 40063, Tucson, AZ 85717.

 ## SPARK CONTROL SYSTEMS.

These govern other systems that advance or retard distributor timing. They enable an engine to burn the air/fuel mixture at exactly the right time. This promotes efficiency and greatly reduces HC, CO and NOx emissions. As a rule, most components don't need maintenance. Check vacuum hoses and wires to ensure they are connected and in good condition.

 ## "CHECK ENGINE" LIGHT.

If this light comes on, *don't ignore it.* In nearly every case, a "check engine" warning is an indication of a problem with, or servicing due, some part of the emissions control system.

 ## AIR INJECTION SYSTEMS, AIR PUMPS, SMOG PUMPS.

These selectively inject fresh air into the exhaust system to aid in the combustion process. This reduces HC and CO emissions. Another system, called a pulse air system, does the same job without using a pump.

Little maintenance is needed on either system. Check drive belt for condition and replace if necessary. Some pumps may have an intake filter that needs periodic replacement. Seal off the pump (cover it with a plastic bag) if the engine compartment is to be cleaned. Liquid infiltration can ruin it.

THERMOSTATIC AIR SYSTEMS.

These supply warm air to the carburetor during cold engine operation and are functional only during cold-engine operation. If your air cleaner's snout has a corrugated hot-air duct leading from it to the intake manifold, you have a thermostatic air cleaner. The inside of the snout also contains a spring and thermostatic-operated door that shuts off outside cold air when the engine is warming and routes the warm air from the manifold to the carburetor. Ducts must be connected and not torn. (See Chapter 2.) The manifold heat riser valve, discussed in Chapter 2, although technically not an emissions device, facilitates engine warm-up.

CATALYTIC CONVERTER: TURNING BAD EXHAUST INTO GOOD AIR.

Although emissions controls do an admirable job at containing pollutants, many still enter the exhaust stream after combustion. To keep these post-combustion emissions from venting directly to the atmosphere, they are converted into less harmful products while still in the exhaust system. Since 1975 the catalytic converter has shouldered this responsibility.

Inside the converter is a catalyst, usually some combination of platinum, palladium or rhodium. Current converters are called three-way because they control the emissions of three combustion by-products: HC, CO and NOx.

As the exhaust gases pass through the hot converter they come in contact with the catalyst and are chemically converted (thus the name "converter") into water and CO_2. Think of the converter as a mini-engine that burns or converts what the first one missed. Converters operate at near 98-percent efficiency and have been a boon to cleaning up exhaust.

On the recent anniversary of the 100-millionth catalytic converter produced by General Motors, engineers estimated that the GM converters alone have "cleaned" 30 million tons of hydrocarbons, 150 million tons of carbon monoxide and 10 million tons of oxides of nitrogen from car exhausts. But they won't do it if they aren't working right.

EPA testing has shown that 3-way catalyst emissions systems deteriorate with age. Although the converters are very durable, they won't last forever. A General Motors study of recent-model used cars with 3-way catalyst systems found that emissions can be as high as 100 times normal if the system is neglected. Don't ignore the converter after the vehicle's 5-year/50,000-mile emission system warranty has expired; that's the exact time you want to be sure it works.

Each time your car is up on a lift for servicing, check the condition of the catalytic converter, muffler and exhaust system. If the converter is dented or torn or loose, it should be repaired or replaced. The catalytic converter is the heart and soul of your emissions system and must be in good repair or almost every hint in this book will do little good.

EVAPORATIVE EMISSIONS CONTROL SYSTEM

Most vehicles that go through state emission control testing are checked by inserting a probe into the vehicle's exhaust pipe that reads the amount of pollutants and unburned hydrocarbons (HC) in the exhaust stream. But Mr. Rich Sommerville, chairman of the committee created by the California legislature to monitor the effectiveness of California's smog check program, notes that "the tail pipe emission test is totally useless in finding problems with evaporative emissions. Exhaust emissions account for only about half of the total hydrocarbon emissions from a vehicle with no emissions control system. Crankcase and evaporative emissions are together almost as large as the exhaust emissions."

ECS=NO EMISSIONS.

On a car with a properly functioning evaporative control system (ECS), evaporative emissions are almost nil. Don't disconnect or tamper with the system—as some mechanics and car owners do. If you do, fuel vapor emissions can be ten times higher than the exhaust HC emissions standard new cars are required to meet.

There are several sources of evaporative emissions that need to be controlled. Fuel vapors that boil off a carburetor when a warm engine is turned off is one source. These vapors are vented from the carburetor to a charcoal canister and are stored there until the car is started. When the engine is restarted, fresh air purges them from the canister and they are drawn into the engine and burned. Other cars store these "hot soak" vapors in the air cleaner. Fuel-injected cars don't have this problem because injectors, unlike a carburetor, aren't vented.

GAS TANK VAPORS.

Another source—perhaps the major one—of evaporative emissions is the gas tank. When it is warmed, due to changes in outside temperatures or heat transfer to the tank from exhaust system components or a hot road surface, vapors fill the tank. In cars equipped with ECS, these fumes are supposed to be vented to a charcoal canister. But if no gas cap is on the filler pipe, or if a vented gas cap is being used, these vapors escape directly into the outside air.

CHARCOAL CANISTER: A VITAL CLEAN AIR GUARD.

The charcoal canister is the main component of the evaporative emissions control system. If it is disconnected or inoperative, gasoline vapors will escape into the air.

Gasoline tank and carburetor vapors are routed through vent lines and stored in the charcoal canister. (See Figure 3 in

Appendix.) When the engine is started, the fumes are sucked out of the canister and burned.

Little service to the system is required. However, the canister is useless if any of its lines are disconnected or the charcoal becomes "deactivated." This can happen if the canister is cracked or damaged or becomes saturated with fuel. In these cases the entire unit should be replaced. Loose or missing lines should be reattached or replaced and the canister checked for proper purging action. Some canisters have a filter that requires periodic replacement or cleaning. Most vehicles built since 1973 use some type of charcoal canister. (For more on reducing evaporative emissions, see Chapter 5.)

A recent survey by the California Highway Patrol found that 6 percent of all evaporative emissions control systems were disconnected, missing or defective. If these vehicles were all in compliance with the law, it's estimated that the HC emissions reductions achieved by the California Smog Check program would be over 30 percent greater. "The number of missing canisters and disconnected or broken vacuum hoses is large enough to be creating a serious emissions problem," says Sommerville.

And this is happening in the state with the nation's most stringent emissions control program. No doubt it's worse in other states.

Here is where individual car owners and the mechanics and technicians who service their cars come into play. The evaporative emissions control system should never be ignored or tampered with, because it plays a major role in reducing overall HC emissions.

EMISSIONS SYSTEM TAMPERING

"No matter how you slice it, the buck stops with us. Whatever they do in Detroit to reduce car emissions, the problem won't get solved if we continue to have a high level of tampering by the car owner."

—JOHN GOODMAN,
State Executive Director,
California Automotive Service
Councils

DON'T TAMPER WITH OR NEGLECT YOUR EMISSIONS SYSTEM.

Don't tamper with the emissions control equipment on your car and don't allow your mechanic to do it. Some car owners mistakenly believe that altering their emissions control systems by disconnecting or bypassing portions of it or installing add-on devices will help the car achieve better performance and economy. There is too much evidence to the contrary: emissions system tampering does more harm than good.

In an Environmental Protection Agency study a number of private repair shop mechanics were asked to alter emissions controls on cars so that the vehicle could get better mileage and performance. (See Figure 4 in Appendix.) However, the results didn't reflect the original intent. The EPA noted that "emissions control system tampering is more likely to hurt fuel economy than to improve it. *Such tampering virtually always makes emissions worse, and can cause deterioration in engine durability. Regular maintenance according to manufacturer specifications improves both emissions and fuel economy."* (Emphasis is mine.)

Tampering with the emissions control system is a no-win proposition. It's one thing environmentally conscious car owners should be adamant about. Cars with computer engine controls are especially vulnerable to tampering. Keep emissions controls in accordance with the manufacturer's specs for best performance and least emissions. Tampering is against the law in most states.

There is an even more mean-spirited kind of emissions system tampering. No sooner than their car passes emissions, some drivers undo portions of it. These drivers cheat the system, cheat themselves and cheat each of us out of clean air. Rigging a car to pass emissions tests and then unrigging it later should carry a heavy fine.

Changing the configuration of the exhaust system is also emissions system tampering because it changes the engine's exhaust back pressure. This can fool some sensors into giving false readings and thus increase emissions. Emissions controls and sensors operate on the premise that the engine is clean and all of its parts are operating efficiently. If this isn't so, then the sensors and emissions system can be tricked into giving false readings with consequent increases in emissions and deterioration in vehicle performance.

Unfortunately, repairing emissions problems can be expensive and time consuming. A study conducted for the EPA by the Radian Corporation involved fuel-injected cars that failed to meet California state emissions tests in 1986. It found that the costs of repairs to bring cars back into full compliance with emissions standards "often exceeded $500 *for parts alone.*" (Emphasis is mine.) The amount of labor required to fix these cars ranged between 2 and 20 hours per car, the study noted.

Radian found that many of the problems were difficult to find and required several hours of time by an expert diagnostician. In the real world, the study noted, it is unlikely that many of the problems would be readily detected and repaired.

One of the main reasons that the systems become so hard and expensive to fix is that owners neglect them. If you check the system periodically, even after the warranty has expired, you are less likely to be confronted with big repair bills.

Technicians capable of diagnosing emissions problems are good people to know. They know how the gases in an engine's exhaust are produced and how to interpret gas analyzer readings. Moreover, they understand the important purpose of emissions control devices and therefore will be among the most sought after repair personnel in the nineties.

Emissions diagnosis and repair, however, takes more than a technician's know-how. Expert equipment is needed. Computer engine analyzers, exhaust gas analyzers, emissions test analyzers, scan tools—all should be part and parcel of a repair facility doing competent emissions work.

But all high-tech equipment isn't created equal. A shop with quality diagnostic equipment will be able to provide quick and accurate emissions diagnosis and effect an accurate repair. And they won't have to take 20 hours to do it.

Many states don't require vehicle "smog" checks. Those that do may exempt certain areas from testing. For example, vehicles in highly populated areas must undergo emissions testing while those headquartered in rural areas are exempt. But whether you live in a city or a small town, in a state that requires emissions testing or one that doesn't, *you* should still make a commitment to eco-driving and eco-maintenance. Let's not wait for state or federal officials to wake up to the reality that *every* car is a polluter no matter where it is driven. Although it may not be contributing to the urban smog problem, it still is polluting the environment.

Abide by the environmental driver's mandate: to drive and maintain your car in such a manner as to make it environmentally neutral—no matter where it is driven.

CHAPTER

4

ECO-DRIVING: ENVIRONMENTAL AWARENESS BEHIND THE WHEEL

". . . [January 1990] imports surged to 9.1 million barrels per day, bringing the import share to an all-time monthly high of 54 percent."

"[The U.S.] probably will be continuously importing well over half of its oil in a few years and perhaps on the order of two-thirds of its oil by 2000."

—CHARLES DiBONA,
President of the American
Petroleum Institute

As automobile owners, we are the undisputed world champions at wasting gasoline and polluting the air. As a nation we need to revive the same fuel-efficient and energy-lean dedication we demonstrated during the past gasoline "crisis," where we proved that as a nation we could conserve gasoline and energy. The most recent statistics released by the American Petroleum Institute (API)—an organization that represents members of the petroleum-based community: oil companies, refiners, gasoline distributors, additive blenders, etc.—showed that as this is being written America is importing more foreign oil than ever before in its history. But the main issue is not that we are, once again, becoming dependent on foreign energy sources, it is that the availability of relatively cheap gasoline has lulled us back into energy complacency. We have forgotten past lessons that helped spare the air as well as conserve fuel. The most compelling reason to conserve fuel now is environmental: The less fuel we use, the less pollutants our cars, trucks and buses emit.

Let's take a refresher course on energy- and pollution-efficient driving techniques. This chapter will outline many driving formulas that will promote minimal tail pipe emissions and maximum fuel economy.

THE CO_2 DILEMMA: TOO MUCH OF A "GOOD" THING

". . . CO_2 emissions are directly proportional to the amount of fuel burned. To substantially limit the CO_2 in exhaust, you have to use less gasoline per mile driven."

—Motor Vehicle Manufacturers
Association (MVMA) press
release

When is a "good" emission bad? One of the main "harmless" constituents produced by the internal combustion process, CO_2, is now being implicated as one of the main gases contributing to global warming and the "greenhouse" effect. Carbon dioxide accounts for about 55 percent of all greenhouse gases. The EPA reports that U.S. emissions of carbon dioxide in 1988 were the highest ever in our country's history. Carbon dioxide, as you probably remember from high school chemistry or biology, is the gas exhaled by every living thing and used by all green things to make oxygen.

Indeed, the main thrust of automotive emissions control programs over the past two decades has been to convert harmful tail pipe pollutants into "harmless" CO_2 and water. It's ironic that the success of automotive emissions controls may have inadvertently helped create another problem.

There is a direct relationship between fuel economy and carbon dioxide production: A more fuel efficient car produces less carbon dioxide per mile traveled than does a gas-guzzler. More miles per gallon = less CO_2 per mile.

The Senate is concerned about vehicle carbon dioxide production and has recently proposed the first bill that would establish vehicular emissions standards for carbon dioxide. This bill is part of the Senate's version of the new Clean Air Act, which is still being considered by both the House and the Senate. It would limit CO_2 emissions to 266 grams per mile starting in 1996. There is much controversy about this proposal, and car manufacturers contend that the only way to meet those standards is to produce lighter cars; however, lighter cars, according to the manufacturers, are unpopular and unsafe.

We *won't* concern ourselves with what may or may not happen to that piece of legislation. We *will* concern ourselves with immediate action to reduce the carbon dioxide emissions of our present vehicles, by learning to drive economically, by maintaining them properly and by considering a more economical vehicle when we trade. Almost every tip in this book, besides helping reduce harmful automotive emissions, will impact CO_2 production.

THE COLD-START:
TOO MUCH OF A BAD THING

 CUT DOWN ON COLD-STARTS.

No time is so emissions-intense as those first few minutes after you start a cold-engine car. There are a number of reasons for this. First, an extra-rich air/fuel mixture is needed. But because liquid fuel won't burn, it must be vaporized. However, cold fuel doesn't vaporize as easily and to get fuel vaporization under cold conditions, more fuel is needed. Much of it is wasted and escapes out the tail pipe as raw gasoline. Because extra fuel is needed to cold-start an engine, we get more pollution.

On newer cars the catalytic converter is also cold. Most must be heated to between 400 and 500°F before they operate efficiently. Until the converter warms, emissions—even in a new car—get a free ride outside.

The oxygen (O_2) sensor on modern cars must also be warm. The O_2 sensor relays exhaust-richness information to the engine's computer, which adjusts the air/fuel mixture accordingly. Until the O_2 sensor is warm enough to work, NOx emissions remain very high.

The standard EPA 26-cycle cold-start emissions test is 7½ miles in length. Experiments conducted by General Motors emphasize just how voluminous initial cold-start emissions are: During the first cycle of the test—1–1½ minutes after a test car was cold-started—about 90 percent of the emissions of hydrocarbons (HC) and carbon monoxide (CO) produced during the entire 26-cycle test were generated.

All carmakers are aware of how much engines pollute when they are cold. Engineers are trying to determine the absolute minimum degree of richness a fuel mixture must have in order to start a car and keep it from stalling. They want to do away with the "comfort factor" of extra (and mostly wasted) fuel. Other pollution-minimizing strategies being considered are to move the catalytic converter closer to the engine so that the heat loss is reduced and the converter can warm faster. Also on the drawing board are preheated catalysts that can be warmed *before* a cold engine is started and thus be immediately effective.

The Swedish carmaker Saab says: "Those first couple of minutes after you have started your car in the morning and begun that daily trek to work can be pretty rough, both on you and your car, and even on the environment. The heater has not yet started and your seat is cold; the car is not really up to it yet and tells you so by running somewhat unevenly. What you don't notice is that your car's exhaust is literally full of pollutants—unburned hydrocarbons, carbon monoxide and nitrogen oxides. . . . The first couple of minutes of driving with a cold engine are responsible for a great portion of all of the pollutants a car emits during its entire driving cycle."

Cold engines are murder on your car and your pocketbook. Now we see they are murder on the air. There is nothing good about a cold-start. Let's look at some ways to reduce the wear, poor fuel economy and high emissions associated with it.

 THINK BEFORE COLD-STARTING.

If the engine is cold, don't move the car if you don't have to. When you come home from work and know you won't be using the car that evening, pull it directly into the garage. Don't wait until after the 10 o'clock news to do it. The short trip into the garage may only take a minute, but it will produce more pollution than hours of freeway driving. And this super-short trip will wear your engine. I've always been intrigued by a study done by the Transportation Department of McDonnell Douglas Aircraft Company that noted "90 to 95 percent of mechanical engine wear takes place in the first ten seconds after a cold start." According to the report, the wear is equivalent to that created by 500 miles of highway driving! Think before you start that cold engine.

 MINIMIZE COLD IDLING.

Don't warm a cold engine by idling. Don't idle more than 15 seconds before putting the car in gear. If the car balks at going so soon after it's started, it's not the car's fault but yours for not keeping it tuned properly. All cars should be able to run without stalling when cold.

When a vehicle is in gear and moving (under road load, engineers would say), the catalytic converter heats up faster and consequently does its job sooner. The faster an engine warms, the quicker the O_2 sensor is activated and the extra-rich fuel mixture leaned.

Cold idling is one of the most fuel-inefficient, and wear- and emissions-intense modes of engine operation. *Cold idling doesn't warm the engine as fast as driving the car.* Most new-car manufacturers recognize this and suggest minimal cold-engine idling for efficiency.

THE CORRECT WAY TO START A CAR

 COLD ENGINE, FUEL INJECTION.

Don't depress or pump the accelerator when starting a cold fuel-injected car. It should start right up—even on the coldest mornings—without depressing the accelerator pedal.

If the car won't start, then depress the accelerator pedal about halfway and hold it there while the turning the ignition key. Don't pump the accelerator; that will only increase the amount of pollution when it finally does start. Consult your owner's manual for the exact cold-starting procedure.

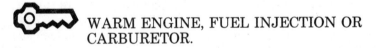 COLD ENGINE, CARBURETOR.

For cold-starting cars with standard carburetors, the accelerator must be depressed, sometimes more than once. This squirts fuel into the manifold and sets the automatic choke for the richer mixture needed. Manufacturers differ on how many times the accelerator should be pumped. Normally, only one or two depressions do the trick. Check your owner's manual for the best method for your car.

WARM ENGINE, FUEL INJECTION OR CARBURETOR.

For fuel-injected *or* carbureted cars: if the engine is warm, don't touch the accelerator. The car should start with only a turn of the key. If it doesn't, depress the accelerator halfway and hold it there while you turn the key.

By following the above cold- and warm-starting routines,

excess raw gasoline is kept from entering the engine. This minimizes unburned HC emissions.

 ## PUSH AND PULL STARTING.

Don't try to push-start or pull-start new vehicles. Most vehicles equipped with automatic transmission cannot be started this way. Vehicles with manual transmissions can suffer severe damage to the catalytic converter.

 ## TAP THE ACCELERATOR.

A cold engine must idle at a higher speed to run smoothly. As the car warms, the engine speed should slow. Tapping the accelerator sharply after the car has been running for about a minute will help lower the idle speed. Electronic sensors on fuel-injected cars usually reduce cold idle speed automatically and require no help from the driver.

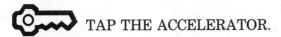 ## CLOSING IN ON THE NONPOLLUTING CAR.

Carmakers are devising ways to neutralize the emissions effect of the cold-start. For instance, Saab's new Climate Adjusted Emissions Control allows the oxygen sensor to operate sooner, thus cutting emissions during cold operation. Where temperatures are 40°F and lower, less fuel is used and HC reductions of 50 percent, and CO and NOx reductions of 20 percent, are being realized. Environmentally engineered innovations like this are leading us closer to the nonpolluting car.

SHORT TRIPS AND CITY DRIVING: BAD NEWS FOR GOOD AIR

According to the EPA, travel habits in the U.S. lean heavily toward driving conditions that give poor fuel economy. U.S. autos accumulate only about 15 to 20 percent of their mileage in trips of 5 miles or less; however, these trips consume more than 35 percent of the nation's automotive fuel because autos operate so inefficiently in short trips. Not only do they operate inefficiently during short trips—on trips of two miles or less, a car may get less than 10 percent of the mileage it does when warm—they pollute more.

 ## START ONLY WHEN READY.

Never start your car's engine until you are ready to go. Many drivers ignore this simple gas-saving and emissions-reducing maxim. How many times a day do you start your engine *before* you are ready to leave?

I think our proclivity to have the engine revving as soon as we get into the car has to do with horses. When our ancestors sat on a horse it was always ready to go; when we get into a car we want the horsepower ready to go. But a horse didn't emit pollution—well, at least not the kind we're talking about—or use gasoline while it waited; a car does.

 ## DON'T TURN ON THE HEAT.

Don't turn the heater on until the engine is warm. This will allow the engine to warm faster. Otherwise, the engine loses some of its precious heat warming up the car's interior. You may have to do without your heater for a few minutes, but is that such a big price to pay for reduced emissions and better fuel economy?

 ## INVEST IN AN ENGINE HEATER.

One of the very best ways to turn your cold-starts warm and eliminate much of the pollution associated with them is to purchase an engine or engine-oil heater for your vehicle. See Chapter 6 for information on these marvelous pollution-reducing, gas-saving and engine-conserving devices.

KNOW YOUR ROUTES.

An EPA "Emissions and Fuel Economy Report" noted that it takes 50 percent more gasoline to drive under urban conditions than on open highways. That's no surprise to car owners and that's why the EPA new-car mileage ratings are higher for highway driving than city. An excellent way of increasing city fuel economy is to know the timing of the traffic lights on your most frequently traveled routes. Most lights operate in the 15-second-to-1-minute range. If you know how long a light stays red or green, you can slow or increase you speed to avoid an unnecessary stop.

DRIVE IN THE "ECONOMY RANGE."

Although city driving consumes much more gas and pollutes more than highway driving, it does offer one efficient mode: Maintain speeds as close as possible to the economical 35–45 mph range. Obviously, on the open highway you can't drive at 35 mph, but in the city there are countless times when you can. It takes less gasoline and produces less emissions to travel at 35–45 mph than it does to go 20 mph. Go faster and you'll get a ticket; go slower and you create pollution.

USE THE WARM CAR.

We have seen that short trips are not much good for anything. Gas mileage is minimal, wear of the engine and other mechanical components is intense and emissions output is highest. Trips of 5 miles or less—a very common trip for the average American driver—don't allow enough time for the car to warm fully and get out of its inefficient operating mode.

There are many two-car families in the United States. Here's a tip that will help both cars last longer and get better gas mileage; it will also cut the emissions output of *both* cars.

Always use the warmest car when you must take a short trip. It sounds so simple, yet it is one of the most effective means of eliminating *unnecessary* automobile pollution. Because the warm car has already paid its warm-up dues (high emissions, poor gas mileage, accelerated engine wear), using it instead of the cold one makes sense.

Why use the cold car and create (unnecessarily) many times the pollution the warm car creates? Use the warm car if you *must* take that short trip. This one act alone can reduce vehicle emissions by millions of tons each year.

 ONE-TRIP SHOPPING.

Combine errands into one trip. Instead of hopping in the car whenever you need something, set aside time to plan your errands. Cluster as many as possible. You'll be surprised at how many unnecessary, smog-producing short trips you'll cut from your daily routine.

 ELIMINATE UNNECESSARY TRIPS.

Is this trip *really* necessary? Must I take the car? Can I bike instead or hitch a ride with a friend? Is a bus or other form of public transportation available? These, and similar questions, are things you should ask yourself before you get into your car. This mini self-interrogation will help cut many otherwise unnecessary trips.

 HIGH-SPEED WORKOUT.

In my book *Drive It Forever* I wrote words that are just as true today: "Perhaps you've heard that taking the car out on the highway once in a while and giving it a 'good run' is beneficial and will help blow out some of the deposits that have built up during city driving. . . . It *is* a very good idea to get your car out on the highway periodically and to give the engine a chance to get fully warmed. The engine coolant must reach a temperature of around 135°F before sludge begins to be boiled off. If highway travel is not on your regular agenda, you should still make it a point to get out and make that highway run. . . . Every trip you take that gives the engine a chance to warm fully is extra insurance against deposit and sludge buildup and the bad tidings they can bring if not held in check."

One of the bad tidings city driving brings is increased tail pipe toxicants. The car must be regularly operated at highway speeds to keep deposits from building up and causing even more pollution. If you are a city driver, an hour or so of high-speed warm-engine exercise once a week will do wonders for your car's constitution and your city's air.

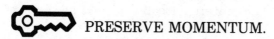 PRESERVE MOMENTUM.

Any car momentum (forward movement) you can conserve is helpful. It takes up to 6 times as much gas (with the subsequent increase in pollution) to get a car moving from a dead stop than from a few miles per hour. Anytime you avoid a complete stop you help clean the air. Preserving momentum is a must for city driving, where many stops are the rule.

> If there is one thing you retain from this entire book, let it be this: that cold-starts and short trips produce more automotive tail pipe pollution than all other driving combined. Anything you do to cut pollution during this time pays increased dividends.

IMPROPER ACCELERATION, DECELERATION AND GEAR SHIFTING: TIMES OF HIGH EMISSIONS

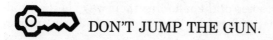 DON'T JUMP THE GUN.

Department of Transportation (DOT) tests have shown that "jumpy starts and fast getaways can burn over 50 percent more gasoline than normal acceleration." And, we might add, they create more than 50 percent more emissions than normal acceleration.

Don't accelerate fully except in emergency or passing situations. Putting the "pedal to the metal" is a pollution no-no. When a full charge of gasoline enters a modern computer-controlled engine, it loses its stoichiometric or "ideal" air/fuel ratio (14.7 parts air to 1 part fuel) and some of the efficiency of the catalytic converter is lost. (See Figure 5 in Appendix.) Much unburned gasoline is routed directly through the muffler and out the tailpipe (older cars) or is simply dumped into the catalytic converter (newer cars).

A warm catalytic converter ideally operates at 98-percent efficiency. But when a load of raw gas is jettisoned into it, efficiency can drop to about 80 percent. Instead of some of the untreated and unburned portions of the gasoline being recycled through the system (engineers call this a "closed loop" system) back into the engine to be burned, much of it remains untreated and goes directly into the outside air.

This whole process is greatly exaggerated if pedal-to-the-metal accelerations are done while the engine and catalytic converter are cold. A major portion of the gasoline is then vented directly into the atmosphere. To goose the car just for the fun of it or to race the car next to you to the stoplight is nonsense. Stay away from full-throttle accelerations—except when absolutely necessary.

GO SLOW ON DUSTY ROADS.

How many times have you seen someone roaring down a dirt road with a long plume of dust trailing after them? In the West it's an all too common sight. Although most of the heavier dust particles eventually settle back to earth, many lighter particles remain airborne, some of them finding their way via the winds into the atmosphere. These fine dust particles add to overall air pollution.

Take it easy on dusty roads. Be respectful of the environment and be aware that vehicle-invigorated dust is definitely a form of air pollution. Just ask someone with allergies. Slow go should always be the rule on dusty roads.

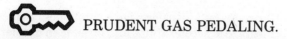 ## PRUDENT GAS PEDALING.

Use this proven economy driving technique to do away with "jackrabbit" starts. Envision an egg between your foot and the accelerator pedal. Accelerate by pushing down in such a manner that the egg won't break. Another way is to pretend there is an apple on the front of the hood. Don't allow it to roll off while you start out. Prudent use of the gas pedal—squeezing it gently—is an easy technique anyone can learn to use.

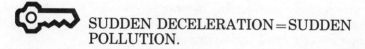 ## SUDDEN DECELERATION=SUDDEN POLLUTION.

There is another emissions-costly habit that is the flip side of sudden full-throttle acceleration: sudden deceleration. Deceleration happens when you take your foot off the gas pedal while the car is moving. Of course, you do this many times each day. And that's fine because when you decelerate correctly, the car's miles per gallon skyrockets.

Sudden deceleration from a high speed, however, is another story. It produces lots of emissions. If you are traveling at 65 mph and abruptly take your foot off the accelerator, high engine vacuum sucks extra fuel. This can cause tail pipe backfiring and will always produce high tail pipe emissions. Older cars are especially prone to pollute under sudden deceleration. On cars with catalytic converters, a sudden flush of unburned fuel can cause the converter to heat up dangerously as it labors to burn the extra fuel. A catalytic converter can be damaged by too many repeat episodes of high-speed sudden deceleration.

Newer cars have devices—GM uses a "decel" valve—that permit extra air to enter the engine when it detects sudden deceleration. Although they do work in cutting deceleration emissions, the driver can help too. Ease your foot off the accelerator gently. S-l-o-w-l-y release the tension and give the engine time to adjust.

Correct acceleration and deceleration techniques reduce emissions: no full-throttle accelerations and no sudden decelerations. The attitude of your right foot is one of the main keys to the automotive pollution solution. What you do with the accelerator pedal, determines, for the most part, what comes out of the exhaust pipe. Treat the accelerator roughly and pollution will be high; treat it gently and you minimize pollution.

Three-time world-champion racecar driver Jackie Stewart sums it up nicely: "My overruling passion has always been to drive as spectacularly as I can in an unspectacular fashion." Stewart stresses that almost every successful racecar driver relies on one main driving technique: finesse. The techniques that give more miles per gallon and less emissions are the exact ones used by great racing drivers.

Respect your car, know its potential and always drive within your and your car's limits. "Light is right," says Jackie Stewart. Those three words can go a long way in helping you become a better eco-driver.

DON'T BE A LUGGER.

Lugging means straining the car in a higher gear when it should be shifted to a lower gear. It occurs with manual transmissions because an automatic transmission will sense the engine's strain and downshift accordingly.

If you feel the car begin to lug, shift to a lower gear fast. This helps reduce the high emissions associated with the internal engine pressures caused by lugging and also prevents possible engine damage. When a car lugs, fuel pours into the engine—a glance at the accelerator will show it is fully depressed—but does little good. Most of it is wasted. There's no excuse for lugging; simply shift to a lower gear at the first sign of engine strain.

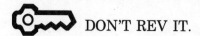 DON'T REV IT.

Revving an engine, especially before turning it off, does absolutely no good. What it does do is flood the engine with raw gasoline that either dilutes the oil, evaporates as HC emissions, or both. Forget vrroom, vrroom: instead, impress your neighbors by showing them how quiet your engine is.

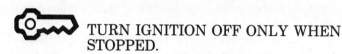 TURN IGNITION OFF ONLY WHEN STOPPED.

Never turn the ignition off while the car is moving. Severe damage to the catalytic converter could result.

IDLIN' AWAY POLLUTION

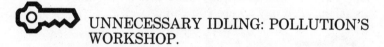 UNNECESSARY IDLING: POLLUTION'S WORKSHOP.

My mother used to say that an idle mind is the devil's workshop. Her son now says that an idling engine is pollution's workshop. Idling has always been a nasty thing; it's one of the most severe modes of engine operation. Besides getting the car absolutely nowhere, it creates lots of pollution. Many cities try to synchronize their stoplights to keep traffic moving just so cars won't have to stop and idle at the lights. The braking effort needed to stop the car and the acceleration required to get it moving again also waste gas.

 IDLE EMISSIONS ARE THE WORST.

If your state is one that requires an emissions test—and all states should—you will notice that emissions "at idle" is always tested. That's because idling produces such high emissions. Making sure your car meets or exceeds state idle emission standards is one way that each state protects the integrity of the air.

 REMEMBER THE 30-SECOND RULE.

There are many ways to reduce idling, and it may be as easy as turning your engine off. It's more fuel- and emissions-wise to turn the engine off and restart it than to let it idle longer than 30 seconds. Depending on its size, an engine uses about a gallon of gas for every 1 to 2 hours it idles. It won't take long to save a gallon of gas and eliminate the nasty by-products that go with burning it.

In addition to producing high emissions, the rich fuel/air mixture needed for idling can cause the catalytic converter to overheat during periods of prolonged idling. Although newer cars have provisions to prevent converter overheating, one of the best ways to avoid it is simply to turn the engine off. Of course, you wouldn't want to turn the engine off if you are in heavy traffic for fear it may not restart. But there *are* many occasions each day where you can.

DON'T IDLE IT; PARK IT.

Drive-up teller lines, fast-food drive-through lines, waiting for a train, waiting for someone in a shopping mall or at home— you can think of many more—all provide excellent opportunities to reduce idling. Better yet, whenever you can, park the car and walk into the places of business. Drive-through lines may be tempting, but they're also serious smog factories.

TURN ASAP.

Take advantage of right-turn-on-red laws. Don't sit there dawd-dlin' and idlin' and pollutin' waiting for the light to turn green. If the way is clear, make your turn and keep moving.

AN IDLE EXCEPTION.

Turn your engine off immediately after arriving at your destination. There is one exception, however. After a long high-speed run, it's better to idle for a minute or so. This helps eliminate any engine "hot spots" and relieves hot fuel vapors that could cause hard starting afterwards. It also helps burn those vapors instead of letting them escape into the atmosphere.

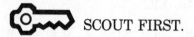 SCOUT FIRST.

Look around your car before getting in. Doing an advance scouting report on the conditions around your car will save you time and gasoline. By noting any problems beforehand, you are better prepared to deal with them once the engine is started.

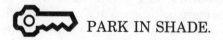 START THE ENGINE LAST.

Be ready to go before starting your engine. Don't start the car and *then* light your cigarette or rearrange packages or buckle the kids in. Do these things first, then start the engine.

OTHER TECHNIQUES

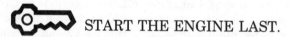 PARK IN SHADE.

Parking in the shade keeps gasoline evaporation to a minimum. On newer cars with closed-to-the-atmosphere fuel systems, gasoline vapors are stored in charcoal canisters. When the car is started, they are sucked into the engine and burned. But on older vehicles, hot vapors vent directly into the air. Shade keeps the car cool and the gasoline in the tank.

 GARAGE IT.

If you have a garage or a carport, use it. In hot, dry or dusty climates a garaged car is impervious to gasoline evaporation. In pre-evaporative emissions vehicles, as much as a quart of gasoline can be lost on extremely hot, windy days if the car is left outside. Shelter from wind and cold will also keep the engine from cooling rapidly. Anything you can do to conserve the engine's heat will help minimize pollution the next time the vehicle is started.

PARK AND WALK.

I've often wondered how much fuel America could save if we didn't have to park "up front." How many times have you seen drivers going round and round in a shopping mall parking lot searching for the perfect parking place? Instead of taking the first available space and shutting their engine off, they tool around the lot oblivious to the fuel they are burning and the pollution they are causing. I imagine billions of gallons of gas could be saved each year and the air could be spared tons of pollutants if only people would give up this nasty and selfish habit.

GO STEADY.

Keep speeds steady on the highway. Emissions at a constant 60 mph are virtually nil. Seesawing back and forth between 50 mph and 65 mph produces more pollution. Varying speeds will also cost you miles per gallon. One study has shown that on the highway, varying speeds by only 5 mph can reduce economy by as much as 1.3 mpg. Steady is the word when on the road.

FORGO THE A/C WHEN POSSIBLE.

Running your air conditioner costs you extra fuel and, because it makes the engine work harder, can increase pollution. Turn the A/C off whenever possible. Use the vents when you can.

DON'T TAILGATE!

It's pollution-dumb driving at best and is very unsafe to boot. Driving too close to the car ahead of you makes you brake and accelerate, brake and accelerate. The car in front dictates how you drive. That's foolish. Don't play the slow-and-go game.

AVOID SUDDEN STOPS.

Quick stops can cause fuel to slosh out of the gas tank or the carburetor bowl.

BE AN ECO-DRIVING FAMILY.

It does only partial good if one member of a family tries to drive environmentally while the others don't. Make a family commitment. Make yours an ecologically and environmentally conscious driving family. Teach *all* members to drive it right, drive it light and drive it clean. Make this book required reading for all licensed drivers.

TOW THE PROPER LOAD.

As you become familiar with this book you'll see that the performance of the emissions control system is affected by customer maintenance, fuel and lubricant quality, tampering, and operating conditions of the vehicle. Here is an operating condition (driving technique) to be aware of: If you pull a trailer or haul heavy loads, be sure you do so within the towing capacities specified in the owner's manual. Trying to pull or haul more than the vehicle is rated can overheat the catalytic converter and shorten its life.

ECO-TRAINING IS NEEDED.

I'd like to see driver training classes restructured to introduce new drivers to eco-driving techniques. I'd also like to see state driver's license tests include a cadre of questions on eco-driving. The more drivers we can make aware, the cleaner the air.

CLEANER IS SAFER.

One statistic that hasn't changed much through the years is the 50,000 or so people killed each year in automobile accidents. As mind-boggling as that number is, I'm even more startled by another number: According to the National Safety Council, a full 85 percent of all those accidents were avoidable.

We have seen that an eco-driver is also an economical, wear-efficient driver who is saving money. But there's even more benefits to eco-driving: safer driving. The eco-driver's car is always in top-notch condition, and the driver is more aware behind the wheel. Cleaner air, better mileage, longer-lasting cars, enhanced safety, money saved—where else will you find such a winning, no-lose combination?

RESPONSIBLE OFF-ROAD DRIVING.

Owners of off-road vehicles (ORVs) should make protection of the environment a priority. Powerful 4x4 ORVs are meant, as their names imply, for use off the main roadways. Considerate ORV owners will inquire about the area they are contemplating driving in before they go and be certain that this type of driving is permitted. 4x4s can destroy pristine forest or desert with just a few passes. Be responsible. Be ecology-oriented. Keep your 4x4 to designated areas and learn how to drive it properly.

All off-road vehicle owners should adhere to safe and ecologically sound driving procedures. A number of carmakers offer off-road driving guides free of charge that highlight proper off-road driving techniques and environmental attitudes.

CHAPTER

5

THE GAS STATION: AN IMPORTANT STOP ON THE ROAD TO CLEAN AIR

"Simply put, we in the petroleum industry know we're part of the environmental problem and we intend to be part of the solution."

—C. J. SILAS,
Chairman & Chief Executive
Officer,
Phillips Petroleum Company

The vast portion of evaporative emissions—the hydrocarbons that escape when gasoline evaporates—are loosed into the atmosphere when we fuel our vehicles. As an engine uses gasoline the fuel level becomes lower. It doesn't take an engineer to figure that out, but something must replace the fuel. Outside air must have a way of getting into the gas tank to fill the vacuum. On older cars, air enters through vent tubes located in the tank or through vented gas caps. But if air can enter the tank, gasoline vapors can escape from it.

Newer-model cars with evaporative emissions control systems keep gas vapors in the fuel system where they belong but still let air into the tank. But even the newer systems can pollute. The next two sections give tips on what you can do to minimize evaporative pollution while pumping gas. The remainder of the chapter deals with finding the best and most pollution-free fuel for your vehicle.

GAS CAPS: GUARDIANS OF CLEAN AIR

I doubt if anyone has ever calculated the amount of evaporative emissions that escape from gas tanks due to loose or incorrect gas caps. It has to be a big number. Here are some ways to make it smaller.

 THE RIGHT CAP.

Gas caps are an integral part of the evaporative emissions control system. But all gas caps aren't created equal. What's good for Peter may be disastrous for Paul; what may work on your Chevy won't on your Ford. Check to see that you have the correct gas cap. A nonvented gas cap used on a vented system can cause serious safety and driveability problems; a vented gas cap used on a closed system allows vapors to escape and may affect the performance of the car.

 CAP IT OFF.

Remember when you would see a car with a rag hanging out of the gas tank filler neck? The owner put it there because he had lost the gas cap or left it at a filling station. It's an open invitation for gasoline to evaporate and dirt to enter the tank. Don't drive around without a gas cap even for a short time.

 REPLACE YOUR CAP.

Check the gasket on your gas cap. Does it look frayed or worn? Are there nicks in the rubber or plastic seal? If it looks questionable, replace the cap. Gas caps aren't expensive, but they play a critical anti-pollutive role.

GASSING UP THE RIGHT WAY

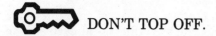 DON'T TOP OFF.

Don't fill the tank to the top. On a hot day the gasoline will expand and leak from the tank, or on cars with the filler hole behind the rear license plate, it will leak out when you go up a hill. Keep the tank a gallon or two below the full mark to ensure that expansion or gravity won't cause spillage.

Although many newer cars have a built-in "safety" space that prevents overfilling, older cars don't. Topping off fosters spilled gasoline. Your car will drive just as well when the tank is a gallon or two below the full mark.

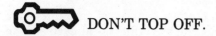 RECAP SPEEDILY.

After you have pumped gas, replace the gas cap fast. If you feel I'm belaboring a point, consider that even from a surface area the size of your filler cap volumes of gasoline vapor can escape in a few seconds. Multiply that amount by some 200 million vehicles that gas up frequently, and you get the point.

There's another compelling reason for not lingering at the gas pump. The EPA has estimated that a person who uses self-service pumps over a lifetime stands a one in 12,500 chance of developing cancer. The faster you replace the cap, the less chance you have of breathing toxic gasoline vapors.

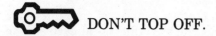 CAP TIGHT.

Screw the gas cap down tight. Newer cars have caps that make a ratchety sound to indicate when they are snugged. Older cars don't have gas caps that chatter. The owner must make sure that the cap is on straight and turned to its fully closed position.

 FILL IT!

The less often you get gas, the less chances of gasoline vapors escaping. Fill the tank—but don't overfill it!—at each stop instead of just pumping a couple of dollars' worth.

 DON'T DRIVE WITH LOW FUEL.

This is just plain common and safety sense. In addition, running out of gasoline can cause engine misfire, which can overburden and even damage the catalytic converter.

 PUMP CAREFULLY.

Be careful when pumping gas. Fast delivery can cause gasoline to backfire out the opening. Best method: set the automatic shut-off on the *slowest* delivery rate or squeeze the handle gently. You don't get any more gas by putting it in fast and you avoid any possibility of environmental contamination. (See Chapter 6 for how you can make a vapor and gas splash guard.)

 ADD YOUR OWN ADDITIVES.

Always buy gasoline at places that do a high-volume business to avoid getting old contaminated fuel. Diesel fuel is particularly susceptible to contamination. If you are planning a trip to Mexico, carry a supply of add-your-own fuel additives. Mexican gasoline, although recently greatly improved, can wreak havoc with the best-tuned automobiles. Cleaners and/or octane boosters, added at each fill-up, will help offset the low octane and dirtiness of the fuel.

CHOOSING THE RIGHT GASOLINE: A POLLUTION SOLUTION

Gasoline has a dramatic say in how much or little your car pollutes. Choosing the right gasoline is one of the most important decisions a car owner can make because some gasolines produce more harmful emissions than others. Finding the right one isn't that complicated.

As we wind our way toward the twenty-first century, nearly all new vehicles will be equipped with fuel injection. Compared to a carburetor, fuel injection is more efficient and produces less emissions. However, fuel injection is more critical to the gasoline's cleanliness than is a carbureted car.

PURCHASE MAJOR BRANDS.

Cheap, off-beat brands will haunt car owners who think they are smart by saving a couple of cents per gallon. Driveability problems result: hesitation and stumble, hard starting, run-on, reduced fuel economy, not to mention increased emissions, are some cheap-fuel symptoms.

Poor-quality fuel doesn't have sufficient detergency. When combined with typical American driving habits—a lot of stop-and-go and long periods when the engine is turned off—the fuel injectors will foul.

Port fuel injectors are located on the hot intake manifold and are subject to a phenomenon called heat soak. After the engine is turned off, the residual heat causes detergent-poor, high-olefin gasolines to break down and bake onto the injector tips. These deposits block fuel flow and cause serious driveability problems. You can't clear the air by using cheap gasoline in your car.

USE A DETERGENT GASOLINE.

Look for a gasoline that advertises its high-detergency or cleanliness properties. There are many of them on the market in every part of the country. Fouled fuel injectors should be a thing of the past—providing you use one of these gasolines. While detergents are a necessary constituent of a good gasoline, the fuel must also contain deposit-control additives that prevent or correct deposit buildup in areas that may affect engine performance and emissions. But all gasolines don't contain the same amount or types of additives and won't give comparable performance. That's why it's necessary to experiment with different brands. Many times, correcting a driveability problem is as easy as filling your tank.

OCTANE: THE RIGHT NUMBER IS IMPORTANT

Besides gasoline cleanliness and detergency, another element plays an important role in emission reduction: octane rating. Simply stated, octane rating (number) is a measure of how well a gasoline resists engine knock.

If the engine is in good mechanical condition, detonation and knock can be caused by using a too low octane fuel. When detonation or knock occurs inside an engine, there will be an accompanying increase in emissions. Current gasolines have octane ratings between 86 and 95. The exact number is posted on the pump. What your car needs depends upon its engine size, compression ratio, whether its turbocharged or not and a number of other factors. For starters, always use the octane recommended in your owner's manual.

 "RUN-ON" RUNAROUND.

If your engine continues to run after the ignition has been turned off—a condition known as "run-on" or "dieseling"—it becomes a virtual pollution machine. Run-on can be triggered by using a too low octane gasoline, by carbon buildup inside the cylinder area or incorrect timing. "Run-on" can be eliminated by a good tune-up, cleaning out of the carbon or simply switching to a higher-octane gasoline.

 GASOLINES AREN'T CREATED EQUAL.

If you're still uncertain about octane, experiment with different numbers until you find one where the car runs smoothly, starts quickly when hot or cold, doesn't run on after the key is turned off and accelerates without hesitation or knock. A slight pinging or subdued knocking (like marbles rolling around in a tin can) on full acceleration is a sign that the octane rating is just about right.

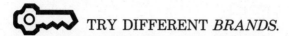 TRY DIFFERENT *BRANDS*.

No two gasolines are exactly the same. Gasolines with identical octane ratings can perform quite differently in your car; it depends on how the gasoline was refined. Try a different *brand* with the same octane you are now using before switching to a higher, more expensive octane. Your car will be the final judge: If it is knocking, clattering, pinging excessively or running on under normal operating conditions, keep trying different brands and/or higher octane. Somewhere the ideal number is waiting. In a survey conducted for Chevron by the research firm R. H. Bruskin Associates, 42 percent of the drivers contacted didn't know the octane rating of the gasoline they purchase. Nearly half of the drivers experienced performance problems with their cars such as stumbling, hesitation, stalling, knocking and pinging, which all have to do with using a gasoline with insufficient octane. Of these, 56 percent said that a tune-up was the proper remedy. But in many cases all that may be needed is using a quality gasoline of correct octane with a deposit-control additive.

 AGING CARS NEED MORE OCTANE.

As cars get older their octane requirements increase and they need a higher-octane fuel to give comparable when-new performance. Keep an ear tuned to your engine and be aware that as the car puts on miles, moving up to a higher octane could be all that is needed to maintain high performance and low emissions.

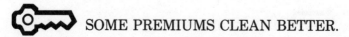 SOME PREMIUMS CLEAN BETTER.

In regard to emissions, there is no difference between premium and regular gasoline. You gain nothing by using premium gasoline in a car that runs well on regular. There is one exception: Some high-test gasolines contain extra fuel system cleaners when compared to regular. These could be helpful if you are conditioning your car or cleaning up dirty fuel injectors.

 LEAD ALERT!

Never use leaded gasoline in a car equipped with a catalytic converter. It will destroy the catalytic converter. Cars have warnings (unleaded fuel only) posted on the dash and on the inside of the gas tank lid as reminders. If you don't know what kind of gas your car takes (leaded or unleaded), find out fast. Consult your owner's manual or ask your mechanic or service station attendant.

 ENGINE DEPOSITS CREATE MORE EMISSIONS.

A number of areas in an engine are suspect to deposit buildup. We have mentioned one of the most prominent, the fuel injectors. In a carbureted car, deposits can build up in the carburetor throttle bodies, the idle circuits, and two main components of the emissions system, the PCV and EGR valves. If deposits form in these areas—and they will if you use cheap fuel—emissions will increase. High-detergent gasolines with a deposit-control additive will keep these areas clean.

We know that the faster an engine warms, the less pollution it produces. The kind of fuel you use has a bearing on warm-up time. Some fuels will allow the engine to warm faster. Environmentally clean, high-detergent gasolines are fast heaters.

ALTERNATE FUELS

 TRY ALTERNATE FUELS.

Alternate fuels produce less emissions than gasoline. There is an array of substitute fuels on which motor vehicles can run,

such as ethanol (grain alcohol), methanol (wood alcohol, usually made from coal or natural gas), compressed natural gas
(CNG), liquefied petroleum gas (LPG), reformulated gasolines,
hydrogen, electricity and solar power. Consult with your mechanic before you decide to use any of these fuels.

OXYGENATES.

Oxygenates are the various alcohols and ethers that can be
added to gasoline. The most common oxygenate is ethanol, an
alcohol made from corn or other vegetable matter. Others are
methanol (wood alcohol) and MTBE (methyl tertiary butyl
ether). When added to gasolines these oxygenates raise the
octane rating and reduce carbon monoxide emissions.

ALCOHOL-BLENDED FUELS.

Methanol- or ethanol-blended (gasohol) gasolines that contain
up to 10-percent alcohol burn cleaner, leave less engine resi-
dues, reduce emissions and give comparable fuel economy
when compared to straight gasoline. So why isn't every driver
using an alcohol-blended fuel? The main reason is that they
aren't readily available nationwide and are more expensive
than gasoline.

The EPA has found that using ethanol blends can cut carbon
monoxide emissions by as much as 30 percent. Pollution-trou-
bled cities like Denver mandate the use of ethanol blends during the winter months.

But older cars with fuel systems that are not alcohol-resistant may be adversely affected by alcohol blends. Newer cars
are alcohol-resistant and most alcohol blends can safely be
used. All car manufacturers caution, however, that if alcohol
fuels cause driveability problems, the owner should switch
back to pure gasoline.

In its 1990 Automobile Warranty, General Motors states:
"The use of oxygenated materials in gasoline can also contribute to cleaner air, especially in those parts of the country where
carbon monoxide and ozone levels are high. Where available,

General Motors recommends use of oxygenated fuels such as . . . ethanol in gasoline."

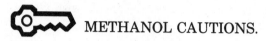 ## METHANOL CAUTIONS.

Whereas every car manufacturer in the world approves of ethanol blends, methanol blends are another story. Some carmakers strictly forbid them, while others allow blends containing up to 5-percent methanol with appropriate amounts of corrosion and cosolvent additives. General Motors says to never "use fuels with more than 5-percent methanol under any circumstances. . . . The use of such fuels are not . . . covered under the New Vehicle and Emission Control System Warranties."

Methanol has other possible drawbacks. The tail pipes of current methanol-fuel vehicles emit more formaldehyde than those of gasoline-using vehicles. Formaldehyde leads to ozone formation and is a probable human carcinogen. Formaldehyde emissions must be controlled before methanol's benefits to clean air can be fully realized.

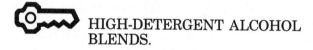 ## HIGH-DETERGENT ALCOHOL BLENDS.

The high-detergent, deposit-control fuels we mentioned previously can also be alcohol-blended. You get the best of both worlds if you can use them in your car: a clean deposit-free engine and a super-clean exhaust.

REFORMULATED GASOLINES

 ## NEW GASOLINE FOR THE NINETIES.

A number of major oil companies (Amoco, ARCO, Citgo, Marathon, Phillips and Shell) are testing "reformulated" gasolines in certain areas of the country. Reformulated gas contains no alcohol or ethers (oxygenates). Instead, the gasoline is reformulated by changing its chemical composition and physical properties to produce less emissions as compared to currently available brands.

Some oil company executives think that reformulated gasolines will pave the way for other alternative fuels like methanol. Other believe it may be an answer in itself. These new fuels may have their greatest impact on older vehicles without catalytic converters. Available data shows that the benefits to new cars with high-tech emissions control systems are minimal.

Some initial drawbacks to the experimental reformulations are a slight decrease in fuel economy and a slight increase in NOx. Benefits include the decrease in other harmful emissions and enhanced catalytic converter life. According to the manufacturers, reformulated gasolines can match oxygenated fuels in emissions efficiency.

Although the future of alcohol blends, reformulated gasolines and other alternative fuels such as compressed natural gas and propane is undecided, reformulated fuels may be the least-expensive clean-air alternative for the simple reason that oil companies already have distribution facilities in place. See Chapter 6 for information on LPG (liquefied petroleum gas or propane) and LNG (liquefied natural gas).

 KEEP TRACK OF GAS MILEAGE.

When you are trying different gasolines, keep an accurate record of the gas mileage each brand gives. Allow at least two fill-ups for each brand. The one that gives the best mileage—if it is a high-detergent, clean gasoline—will usually be the best one for your car. If all brands are nearly equal, you might let price be the determining factor.

 FIGURE YOUR MPGS.

Here's how to figure your gas mileage. Jot down the speedometer reading to the nearest mile whenever you fill the gas tank. Let's say it reads 8,510. At your next fill-up, mark down the mileage reading again and also record the number of gallons of gas purchased. We'll use 8,760 and 10.2 gallons. Now subtract the previous reading (8,510) from the current one (8,760) and get 250 miles traveled. Now divide that figure by the number of gallons used: $255/10.2 = 25$ mpg. Our gas mileage for that fill-up is 25 mpg.

 THE ULTIMATE CRITIC.

The consumer's vehicle will always be the ultimate critic of gasoline quality. Different batches of gasoline in the same geographical area can differ enough to make a difference in how the car runs and performs. Remember that renewing proper performance and reducing emissions could be as easy as moving to the gas station across the street.

CHAPTER

6

AUTOMOTIVE PRODUCTS FOR "GREENER" CARS

One of the best ways we can clean up the air is to replace all vehicles made before 1983, the year when effective emissions controls were put in place, with later models. But many consumers, for economic and other reasons, may not want to part with their older cars and trucks. The newsletter *Concerning Cars* estimates that it won't be until the year 2000 that the national fleet will consist of mostly 1983 or newer vehicles.

Keep the 83–83 rule in mind: according to GM chairman Roger Smith, cars built before 1983 produce 83 percent of the pollution emitted by all cars on the road. That's a powerful incentive to trade up to a later model.

Some automotive products can help cut emissions, boost gas mileage and assist you at being a better eco-driver. But others, while claiming to do some or all of the preceding, are a waste of money.

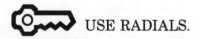 USE RADIALS.

Radial tires are one of the greenest automotive products. Radial tires give better gas mileage—up to ten percent better—when compared to bias or bias-belted tires. That alone should be reason enough to use them. They are also safer, last longer and pollute less.

Tires pollute? According to the California South Coast Air Quality Management District, "radial tires produce less air-damaging particulate matter per mile traveled than bias-ply tires do." As a tire wears, the tread has to go someplace. It goes into the air. Because radial tires last longer, they don't chuck as much of themselves into the air per mile traveled.

 AVOID SHORT-TREAD-LIFE TIRES.

Stay away from those high-performance short-tread-life tires. Tires that wear fast pollute more. Look at the treadwear rating of the tire before purchasing it. It's printed on the tire's sidewall. A rating of 250, for instance, means the tire's tread will last 2½ times longer than a tire rated 100. Environmentally concerned drivers will choose tires with treadwear ratings of 200 or more.

GAUGE TIRE PRESSURE.

A tire pressure gauge is a must for eco-driving and eco-maintenance. We talked about the many benefits of keeping tires inflated to maximum pressure in Chapter 2. An accurate tire pressure gauge isn't expensive (less than $5) and no ecology-minded driver should be without one.

VACUUM GAUGE.

I have long been a fan of the vacuum gauge. You might call it an "anti-pollution" gauge. It measures engine vacuum: the higher the reading, the more efficient the engine's operation. It can teach you how to drive economically, tell you when a carburetor is too rich, detect a manifold leak or obstruction in the exhaust system, spot engine problems before they become major or indicate when to downshift. In short, it's a jack-of-all-trades gauge. Vacuum gauges can be purchased in the $10–$30 price range.

MONITOR THE RPMS.

A tachometer measures engine revolutions per minute (rpms). Once a hot rod innovation, it is now standard equipment on many new cars. By shifting at the proper engine rpm (it's in your owner's manual) you'll boost mpgs and never lug the engine.

A fast-idling engine wastes gas; a slow-idler could be polluting needlessly. A tachometer will tell you exactly how fast the engine is turning at all times and you can adjust engine rpm if required.

AVOID THE HYPE.

Don't be sucked in by advertisements for automotive gadgets that promise gasoline savings and cleaner air. Many worthless "gas-saving" gadgets are being resurrected under the "good-for-the-environment" banner. These products, now dressed in the new clothes of "green" consumerism, still don't work. If something promises a miracle, you can bet it will be a miracle if it works.

More often than not, these gadgets defeat the manufacturer's intent; that is, they change the parameters of the engine's operation and usually make things worse instead of better. They can be quite harmful to computer-controlled fuel-injected cars and most always will result in an increase in emissions.

A number of years ago the Environmental Protection Agency (EPA) tested more than 50 of these so-called gas savers. Their general conclusion: "No increase in fuel economy noted." Here is a list of some of those tested:

Mark II Vapor Injector   Aquablast
Turbo Vapor Injector   Wyman Valve
SCATPAC   Ball-Matic
Franz Vapor Injector   Berg
Econo-Mist   Econo-Jet Idle Screws
ADAKS Vacuum Breaker   Econo-Needle
Air Jet   Landrum Mini-Carb

Landrum Retrofit
Mini Turbocharger
Monocar HC Control
Peterman
Pollution Master
Turbo-Dyne GR Valve, EI-5
Johnson, NGR No. 1
Folfite Upgrade
Sta-Power
Stargas
Technol G
Val-Do Combustion Cleaner
  and Power Lube
Verb 10
Environmental Fuel Saver
Hydro-Catalyst Precombus-
  tion Catalyst System

Analube
Tephguard
BIAP
Magna Flash
Paser Magnum
Special Formula Advance
  Springs
Lee Exhaust and Fuel
  Gasification EGR
Electro-Dyn Superchoke
Filtron Urethane Foam Air
  Filter
Lamkin Fuel Metering Device
Smith Power and
  Deceleration Governor
Malpassi Filter King

There are a lot more; these are just some the EPA has tested. The next time you read a magazine ad about one of these miracle gadgets, toss your wallet to the nearest family member. Then take them out for a nice meal on the money you saved. You'll get a lot more mileage and less pollution from a full stomach than from a tank of wishful thinking.

 DON'T BUY A/C RECHARGE KITS.

Most car owners shy away from working on their air conditioners. The ones that do usually top off the freon with a kit purchased from an auto-parts store. Don't try to recharge the A/C yourself. This job should be left to the professionals. The store-bought kits are almost guaranteed to leak freon. A leftover, half-full can will eventually leaks its contents into the air. You won't find auto refrigeration recharge kits on my "green" list.

 BRAKES SHOULD BE ASBESTOS FREE.

Popular Science magazine recently reported that within three years almost all brake pads and shoes will be free of asbestos.

Currently, about one half of all aftermarket brake pads and shoes contain this toxic substance. Because of an EPA directive, new cars built after 1993 will no longer be permitted to use asbestos in their brakes, and aftermarket shoes and pads sold after September 1996 must be asbestos-free.

You don't have to wait until 1996. If your car is in need of brake shoes or pads, prior to committing to the work determine if the shop uses asbestos-free brake pads or shoes. If they don't, find one that does. It's an easy way you can keep these cancer-causing materials out of the air we breathe.

HAVE A BUMPER STICKER MADE.

Your sticker could say something like "This is an environmentally neutral vehicle" or "I drive environmentally" or "I'm an eco-driver." Maybe drivers that see it will want to follow your cue.

"THINK CLEAN."

Years ago when I wrote *How to Get More Miles Per Gallon* I asked readers to "Think Economy" when they got behind the wheel. I even offered free "Think Economy" stickers to put on the dash. The visual reminder reinforced economy driving habits. It's easy to print the words "THINK CLEAN" or "DRIVE CLEAN" on a piece of paper and tape it to your dash. It will have a similar effect.

SPREAD THE WORD.

I'd like to see businesses volunteer to put up signs at drive-in lanes that tell customers to turn their engines off if idling is to exceed 30 seconds. These signs could save a lot of gas and spare the air. "Place transmission in neutral" signs posted at long stoplights during the summer months might also be helpful.

 RECYCLE USED MOTOR OIL.

Easy-change oil kits allow do-it-yourselfers to safely drain and transport used oil. Old motor oil is drained into a kit-supplied pan where it runs into a sealable bag. The kits hold up to 6 quarts of oil and a filter and claim to be mostly recoverable/recyclable.

But some of the plastic bags may not be biodegradable, in which case the car owner should make provisions to either pour the old oil from the bag into an acceptable container and *then* dispose of it, or, if the disposal site accepts noncontainered oil, dispose of the oil and take the bag home to reuse.

A number of major automotive-supply and retail stores now accept used oil from do-it-yourselfers. Check those in your area or look in the yellow pages under "Oils—Waste" or "Recycling."

ENGINE HEATERS REDUCE EMISSIONS.

For over fifteen years I have praised the beneficial aspects of engine warmers and engine oil heaters. These devices keep the engine, engine coolant or motor oil warm while the car is parked overnight. When the vehicle is started in the morning, the engine is already "prewarmed." Much of the wear and tear caused by a cold start is eliminated, as is the terrible fuel inefficiency of that period (sometimes as little as 1 mpg!).

But what no one appreciated until now is that by prewarming the engine, an engine heater greatly reduces the amount of pollution. An engineer I talked to heartily endorsed engine heaters as one of the very best things a consumer could add to their cars to help cut automotive tail pipe emissions.

Engine heaters come in a variety of shapes and forms. A tank heater fits into a radiator hose and heats and circulates the coolant. An oil dipstick heater warms the oil so it can lubricate more thoroughly. It temporarily replaces the car's normal dipstick. Magnetic heaters clamp onto the bottom of the oil pan and do the same thing. Aftermarket engine heaters range in price from about $10 to $30. Oil warmers can be purchased for as little as $6.

Many newer cars have outlets built into the engine block that accommodate a manufacturer-made engine heater. If you are considering a new car, ask whether an engine heater is available. Before you purchase an aftermarket engine heater, you may want to check to see if your present car has an outlet for a factory-option engine heater.

I don't understand, what with all the fuss over the new Clean Air Bill, why engine heaters aren't standard equipment on every new car. They aren't that expensive and would probably reduce automotive pollutants better than the expensive new mandates with which manufacturers must comply. Maybe it's too simple a solution for the political process: Why require something that doesn't cost much but will reduce vehicle emissions substantially, when something more costly can be mandated that won't do as good a job?

"ENERGY CONSERVING II" MOTOR OILS.

According to the American Petroleum Institute (API), the first generation of these oils, know as Energy Conserving I, "produced a fuel economy improvement of 1.5 percent or greater over a standard reference oil in a standard test procedure." Many high-quality oils are now designated "Energy Conserving II," and every car owner in the United States should be using them. This second generation of fuel-efficient oils can produce a 2.7 percent or greater increase in fuel economy when compared to non–energy conserving oils of the same viscosity.

Because these oils can save fuel, their use should be universal. We have seen that anything we do to increase fuel economy will lessen tail pipe pollution and cut carbon dioxide. The next time you change the oil, ask for an "Energy Conserving II" oil.

ADD SOLID LUBES.

Solid lubricants are a class of oil supplements that, like the Energy Conserving II oils, boost the car's gas mileage and reduce pollution if used regularly. Solid lubricants enhance the motor oil's ability to reduce friction. The car runs more efficiently and wear of critical engine components is reduced.

The three most common solid lubricants are graphite, molybdenum disulfide (moly) and polytetrafluoroethylene (PTFE). Adding any one of these to the oil at oil change time is a positive ecological move. No doubt you've seen magazine or TV ads for some of these products.

Some solid lubricants work better than others. If the container says "Shake Well Before Using," the product probably isn't properly suspended and much of it will settle out in your engine. If you must shake it, put it back on the shelf.

For more information about energy-saving solid lubricants, send a business-size, self-addressed stamped envelope to The Mileage Company, P.O. Box 40063, Tucson, Arizona 85717.

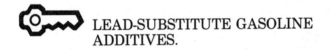 ## LEAD-SUBSTITUTE GASOLINE ADDITIVES.

These gasoline additives protect valve parts on older cars from wear. That's one of the jobs leaded gasoline used to do. But with leaded gasoline becoming harder to find, more owners of older cars are turning to lead-substitute additives. Even where leaded gasoline is available, environmental drivers of older cars may opt to use these additives in combination with unleaded gasoline, instead of using leaded gasoline alone. That helps keep poisonous lead out of our air.

Since the EPA ordered its phaseout, the lead content of leaded gasoline has dropped from a high of about 2.5 grams per gallon (gpg) to the current maximum allowable 0.1 gpg.

Although the EPA has no final plans for a complete phaseout of lead from gasoline, owners should be aware that the current 0.1 gpg requirement is the maximum allowed by law; in reality, gasoline refiners may add far less. So the benefits of using currently available "leaded" gasolines may be quite minimal. That's another reason to switch to the more environmentally safe lead-substitute additives.

DON'T USE REAL LEAD ADDITIVES.

All ecology-minded drivers should boycott lead-substitute additives that contain *real* tetraethyl lead. It's interesting that one of these products, advertised in an *automotive* products magazine, displays a "Warning to California Motorists" that reads: "For boat engines only. Unlawful for sale or use in California as a fuel additive to any motor vehicle. Will severely damage motor vehicle catalytic converters . . ."

Another warning to California consumers states: "This product contains a chemical known to the State of California to cause cancer, birth defects or other reproductive harm."

If it's harmful to California cars and residents, how about the cars and residents of the other 49 states? Read the label: if it contains real lead, put it back.

CLEAN FUEL INJECTORS ARE A MUST.

Fuel injector and fuel system cleaners are useful products. They are extra insurance that the injectors and other parts of the fuel system will stay clean. I suggest that in addition to the clean high-detergent gasolines we discussed in Chapter 5, a container of fuel-injector cleaner be used at every third fill-up.

MAKE A GAS VAPOR AND SPLASH GUARD.

You can make a combination gasoline splash and vapor guard to use when filling the tank. Using a plastic coffee can lid, cut a circle slightly larger than the diameter of the gas cap. Then cut a hole in the center of the plastic disc large enough—but not too large—so the gas pump nozzle fits snugly through it.

Before filling the tank, slide the vapor/splash guard over the end of the pump nozzle and insert the nozzle into the filler neck, snugging the guard against the filler neck. That's all there is to it. The guard will help keep gasoline vapors from escaping into the atmosphere and gasoline from spitting out of the tank. Do not use this device in Stage II gas pumps.

BUY THE MOST ENVIRONMENTAL VEHICLE.

New- and used-car buyers should consider the most efficient and practical car they can afford. We know that the more efficient the car is, the less harmful emissions it produces. Careful consideration should be paid to the vehicle's estimated EPA mileage numbers. You can obtain a free copy of the "Gas Mileage Guide" that contains mileage numbers for every car sold in the U. S. by writing to Gas Mileage Guide, Consumer Information Center, Pueblo, Colorado 81009. You can also pick one up at new-car dealers. But be an eco-driver: call first, to make sure they have them in stock.

Used-car buyers would be smart to look up the "when-new" mileage ratings of the used car they are considering.

Like never before, choosing a good used car is a great challenge. Price and condition continue to be major considerations, but we should also be concerned with the vehicle's emissions performance.

JUNK OLD POLLUTERS.

When you get rid of your older car and trade up to a newer, more efficient model you help clean the air—providing the vehicle you traded in isn't pawned off on someone else who doesn't give a whit about car care. Leave your old car in the best condition possible. But if your old car is a polluter, do the air a favor and offer it to a junkyard. It may cost you a few bucks, but don't you think breathing is worth it?

Maybe Uncle Sam could offer tax write-offs for car owners who do just that? It would be easy to set up a system based on the car's current retail value. The polluter is off the road and the owner gets compensated for it.

Each older vehicle that is scrapped and replaced by a newer, more emissions-efficient one makes a significant contribution to hydrocarbon and ozone reduction. Some estimates show that by the year 2000, fleet turnover will account for about a 38-percent reduction in vehicle hydrocarbon emissions, with similar reductions projected for carbon monoxide and nitrogen oxide.

 ## CHECK EMISSIONS BEFORE YOU BUY A USED CAR.

Never buy a car without looking at its most recent emissions test result. If it isn't available, ask the owner if you can have the car inspected. Emissions are a clue to the car's general health, so this information helps you in more ways than one.

 ## STAY AWAY FROM THE OIL BURNERS.

A car that uses oil, especially a catalytic converter model, can be made to pass emissions, but it will deteriorate rapidly as the burning oil begins to foul emissions system components.

If the O_2 sensor, for instance, becomes fouled with oil its readings won't be accurate and the engine's operation will be affected. Just disabling this one sensor will increase NOx emissions manyfold.

The catalytic converter converts unburned gasoline into water and CO_2. Although most converters are also very good at treating smoke from burning oil, a constant barrage of it can diminish the converter's efficiency and shorten its working life, especially if the oil is inferior quality. And what kind of oil do people usually put in oil burners? You guessed it, inferior-quality oil.

 ## CONSIDER DUAL-FUEL SYSTEMS.

According to the American Gas Association (AGA), in 20 years, about a million cars on the road will be powered by natural gas.

AGA estimates that vehicles powered by natural gas (NGVs or natural gas vehicles) can reduce carbon monoxide car emissions by up to 82 percent. Even more importantly, using natural gas instead of gasoline could cut the production of reactive hydrocarbons, which contribute greatly to ozone production. AGA estimates that reactive hydrocarbons could be cut up to 87 percent when compared to those produced by gasoline-powered vehicles.

LPG (liquefied petroleum gas or propane) and LNG (liquefied natural gas) have been shown to be superior to conventional gasolines in cleanliness. A number of companies across the U.S. now offer engine conversions that make use of these fuels possible. Dual-fuel systems allow you to use either gasoline or propane with the flick of a switch.

Vehicles equipped with dual-fuel systems emit less pollution. Additional benefits are a cleaner engine and longer engine life. Because there are few gasoline-generated contaminants, the motor oil stays cleaner longer.

Dual-fuel systems, although rather expensive, are environmental winners. They should be seriously considered by car owners willing to put their bucks where their pollution used to be.

 BE A CAUTIOUS "GREEN" CONSUMER.

The "green" consumer revolution isn't limited to products for the home or table. It has found its way into the automotive market also. Look for environment-safe products when shopping for car-care products. Biodegradable and recyclable automotive products that work just as well as nonbiodegradable and nonrecyclable ones are available *now*.

Many of these products are packaged in biodegradable containers that can be recycled or taken to a landfill. Although they may cost a bit more, they are worth it.

A few of the currently available car-care products include engine cleaners, car cleaners and polishes, in-a-can flat tire fixes and more. Look for these products in a special section of auto parts stores or ask a salesperson.

BEWARE OF ENVIRONMENTAL HYPE.

There are many products that the makers claim to be environmentally safe but that in reality aren't. Some manufacturers are hopping on the bandwagon because they see profit in the green revolution. Many of these same companies weren't concerned about clean air or contamination before it came into vogue. It's still caveat emptor—let the buyer beware. Check any item closely that claims to be "green." Determine if it really is before you buy.

CHAPTER

7

RECYCLING AUTOMOTIVE
PRODUCTS

"As good corporate citizens, Chrysler has made the choice to use only recyclable thermoplastics on future body panels."

—B.E. SWANSON,
executive engineer of materials
engineering at Chrysler and
current chairman of the
Automotive Composites
Consortium

"Basically, the car you are producing has become, due to the inability or difficulty in landfilling the fluff, unrecyclable."

—ROBERT K. WAXMAN,
Waxman Metals Group,
a recycling firm in Hamilton,
Ontario

Many of the products we use to keep our vehicles operational can be recycled after their useful life is up. Any auto-dismantling yard will also attest to the fact that many parts of the automobile itself are recyclable.

RECYCLABLE VEHICLES.

Many recycling centers are loath to burden their lots with plastics from newer-model cars because of their virtual indestructibility. These plastics don't biodegrade, nor do they recycle easily. But we may be seeing recyclable cars in the not-too-distant future. A number of carmakers are investigating the concept of a totally recyclable vehicle. Even today, some manufacturers are using recyclable materials in door panels and headliners in place of the hard-to-kill or impossible-to-recycle plastics.

BMW is building a plant in Bavaria where it will disassemble cars and reuse what is recyclable. Volkswagen AG is constructing a similar plant. The aim is 100-percent recyclability by the year 2000. But in the meantime, here are some recycling ideas that will pay off in big clean-air dividends now.

DON'T TAKE OLD TIRES TO A LANDFILL.

Landfill operators hate old tires. They have an uncanny ability to work themselves to the top of the landfill no matter how deeply they are buried.

When you buy a new set of tires, trade your old ones in at the tire dealership. (See Chapter 6 on buying environmentally sound tires.) If they have good casings (recappable sidewalls) they are worth money and can be recycled. Even if the tires are beyond recapping—and they shouldn't be, for you shouldn't be driving on unsafe tires like that—ask your tire dealer to dispose of them properly.

Old tires pose a serious recycling problem. We go through roughly 200,000,000 of them each year. There is some promise that these tires can be shredded and used for making other products. But as of now, the problem of what to do with old tires is largely unresolved. But one thing we do know: It's not wise to overburden our landfills with these pop-to-the-top artists.

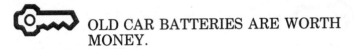 ## OLD CAR BATTERIES ARE WORTH MONEY.

Sell yours for a couple of bucks to a company that recycles used batteries. Both you and the environment benefit. Look under "Battery Repairing and Rebuilding" in the yellow pages for names.

You can trade your old battery in when you buy a new one. Many larger stores accept trade-ins and might even give you a couple of bucks for the old lead. Either way, you are putting the old battery to good and proper use.

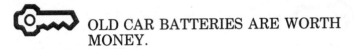 ## RECYCLE USED MOTOR OIL.

A recent Washington State Department of Licensing newsletter noted that "more than five million gallons of used oil are dumped in Washington State every year, carrying toxic contaminants and carcinogens into our environment. Used oil pollutes our streams and lakes and even seeps into the ground to pollute drinking water." And this is in Washington, one of our most environmentally attuned states.

Don't dump old oil onto the ground, down the sewer or drain, or in a lake or stream. Washington's Department of Ecology, for instance, has a toll-free hot line (1-800-RECYCLE) to contact to get the location of the nearest recycling center. Your state may offer a similar service. Remember to keep old motor oil in a separate container and don't mix it with other disposable liquids. (See Chapter 6 for more information on oil disposal.)

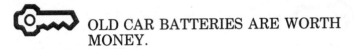 ## RECYCLING COOLANT IS COOL.

Just as used motor oil shouldn't be scattered haphazardly, neither should old antifreeze/coolant. Although coolant is not as hazardous to the environment as used motor oil, it should be disposed of properly. Like used motor oil, coolant should be placed in a leak-proof container and taken to a recycling center or a licensed disposal site. (Check the yellow pages under "Recycling Services" or call your county health department for a location.)

☞ "DRY OUT" SCRAPPED VEHICLES.

We may see more and more car owners scrapping their old cars instead of pawning them off on other drivers. If you choose to do so, have the air-conditioning system professionally evacuated before the car is scrapped. That way the freon won't escape into the atmosphere while the car is sitting in a wrecking yard.

This also applies to cars that are wrecked or damaged. If they are going to their final resting place, their A/C systems should be evacuated beforehand. We know that freon vigorously attacks the ozone layer and that gasoline vapors aren't good for the air. The gasoline tanks on discarded vehicles should be emptied before they are put to sleep. Indeed, any scrapped vehicle should be put away totally "dry."

☞ LITTERING IS POLLUTING.

Cars may toss stuff out their exhaust pipes, but they don't throw diapers and bottles and cigarettes out of the windows—drivers and passengers do. I once saw a cartoon that showed a family heaving a bag of trash out a car window. The driver was saying, "Don't worry, it's biodegradable." Sadly, trash tossers seem to be a major force in our society.

Let's keep our trash in our cars and dispose of it properly—most all bottles and cans are recyclable—and not along our roadways. Each car should have a trash container. A large paper bag or a reusable plastic container is ideal. They can be extra handy on those long vacation trips when more trash is generated.

Cans, bottles, fast-food polystyrene containers and "disposable" diapers take years to biodegrade. Visual pollution can be just as offensive as the other kind. Those drivers who clutter up the beauty of our roadways make a strong statement about how they feel about the rest of the environment.

ALTERNATE TRANSPORTATION: A MAJOR KEY TO CLEAN AIR

EPA studies have shown that if only one person were added to the average commuter load, 50,000,000 gallons of fuel could be saved—*daily!* There would be an equally impressive reduction in automotive emissions. Using alternate means of transportation may be the single best way to clean the air.

BE KIND TO THE PEDALER

When was the last time you rode a bicycle? That long ago? OK, how long has it been since you owned one? Even longer, you say.

What brings all this to mind is an incident that occurred recently when I was driving to town. A bicyclist was going in the same direction as I was, keeping as far to the right as possible, hugging the curb as best he could. A driver a few car lengths ahead of me wasn't satisfied with the bicyclist's demeanor, however, obviously feeling that the bike had no right to slow him down (these roads are for cars, you know!).

The driver took out his pent-up aggression on the slow-moving bicycle, literally running the pedaler off the road, sending him careening over the curb and almost crashing into a nearby wall. The bicyclist raised a clenched fist as the car whizzed on. The driver of the car, grinning, countered with a raised finger.

Bicycling friends of mine say incidents like this are fairly common, and those who rely on a bicycle as their main means of transportation say they look at every driver as a potential assassin, an adversary in a battle they can't possibly win. All have had close calls; caution is the byword at all times. On streets where there is no bike path, they must join the mainstream of traffic, and most do so with great trepidation. Many use side streets whenever possible to avoid heavy traffic. They are all keenly aware that in a one-on-one confrontation with a car, they don't stand a chance.

Why all this talk about bicycles in an automotive book? Mainly because the number of bicycles increases each year, and more and more of them are sharing the roads with cars and trucks. Although most bicyclists use designated bike paths whenever possible, the paucity of these protected areas forces them to use main traffic arteries at times. These are times when we, the pilots of those moving boxes of plastic and steel, should go out of our way to be extra careful when approaching a bicyclist.

Every driver on the road owes something to every bicyclist: Bicycles aren't polluting the atmosphere with carbon monoxide, particulate matter, unburned hydrocarbons, lead, nitrous oxides, poisons, ad nauseam; they aren't adding to our tax burden by beating up on our roads; and each one on the road makes your own town a much better place to live and breathe.

Bicycles are the ultimate mileage machine: unlimited mileage on zero gallons of gasoline, zero quarts of oil. They are quiet, clean, relatively fast, nonpolluting, good for you and me. And if you own both a car and a bike, each time you use your bike you extend the effective life of your car.

Occasionally you may become a bit irritated when a bike is in front of you and you have to slow down, but that is a small price to pay for what we are getting in return. A bicycle benefits everyone; a car, just its owner.

So the next time you encounter a bicycle, slow down, smile, be extra careful, extra courteous. Remember, the gas it's saving could be yours; the air it's not polluting is everyone's.

URBAN ALTERNATIVES

Mexico City has one of the world's worst urban smog problems, and experts say that private motor vehicles are responsible for more than 50 percent of the pollution. Recently the air quality deteriorated to a point where a system was devised to limit the use of the 2.5 million vehicles that call Mexico City home. Colored stickers were issued to car owners. On the day of the week their color was posted, they weren't allowed to drive. That kept 500,000 vehicles per day off the streets. And it made a difference. After only 4 months, air pollution was reduced by as much as 15 percent. But incredibly, new-car sales rose dramatically during the months the ban was in effect. People were buying a second car so they wouldn't have to use public transportation on the day their primary car's sticker was posted.

 GIVE UP YOUR CAR OCCASIONALLY.

If you don't drive your car, it can't pollute. Anytime you take the bus or train or subway, or ride-share or carpool or vanpool, you don't pollute. So why aren't more of us using public transportation or taking advantage of the numerous ride-matching programs set up by various city and county transportation departments? Like the Mexico City car owners, we hate to be without our cars. We don't like being inconvenienced. Some of us feel impotent without our personal means of transportation—we can't make a statement riding a bus! We feel cheated if we can't go anywhere we want anytime we want to.

I wonder if it really is *that* inconvenient to find another way to work at least once a week, or is our "freedom" more important? For now, individuals are free to resolve these issues in their own way. If air quality continues to deteriorate, we may lose some of that freedom of choice.

The public good must occasionally be placed before individual priorities. This is one of those times. Isn't it worthwhile to give up a bit of that freedom once in a while in order to have clean air? Carpools, vanpools, public transportation—there are numerous ways other than one person/one car to get to work. Whenever you use an alternate means of transportation, you relieve freeway congestion too.

 ## THE MORE THE MERRIER.

The more people in the carpool or vanpool, the better. The savings in money, fuel and air quality are compounded when additional people are added to the pool. Alternate transportation cuts down on car repairs and commuting costs and, not to be ignored, the stress level of all participants is lowered considerably.

Each time you *don't* use your car you are adding miles to the top end of its odometer reading. If you carpool 60 miles just one day a week, that adds up to a savings of over 3,000 miles per year. That's essentially 3,000 extra miles you can use your car for. A nice bonus for doing something that already is saving you money and making a major contribution to cleaner air.

She would never think of herself as either a conservationist or an environmentalist, yet she may be the quintessence of one. She would never think that her means of transportation for 80 years had anything to do with clean air. It was how people like her got around. It wasn't out of necessity but out of choice.

My aunt Stella was, and still is, the quintessential public transportation user. To my knowledge, Aunt Stella owned only one or two cars in her lifetime. There's an old picture of me standing on the running board of a 1941 Chevy. A bit more clear are memories of a 1951 Dodge. But since then, it's been buses and streetcars, whether across town in Pittsburgh or heading south to Florida.

Why this reminiscence about my favorite aunt? If each car owner would just have a little more Aunt Stella in them, the air would be a lot cleaner, our oil import quotas would drop significantly and our roads would be a lot less congested. When they dole out the awards for conservation or environmental friendliness, Aunt Stella and the many like her should be at the head of the line.

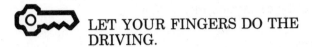 ## LET YOUR FINGERS DO THE DRIVING.

The telephone an alternate means of transportation? Sure. Using the telephone has to be one of the most emissions-efficient driving techniques there is. Use the phone book and phone *before* you hop in the car. Make sure the store is open or has the item in stock or that your friend is home. Many pollution-causing short trips can be avoided by using the phone first.

 ## USE OLD-FASHIONED LOCOMOTION.

How about the world's oldest means of transportation, plain old walking? We know that walking is good for us. Walking is good for the air also. Walk instead of drive whenever you can and you do a lot for yourself and the environment.

CHAPTER

IT'S UP TO YOU

You now hold the keys to clean air. By striking at the heart of the pollution problem—our vehicles—we will make the greatest gains in the fight for clean air. There are many things you can do to clean up automotive pollution: practice eco-driving and eco-maintenance, recycle used automotive products, buy only ecologically sensible automotive products (particularly gasoline and oil), make regular use of the wondrous varieties of alternate transportation and more. It's now up to you. These ideas do little good if they remain stuck to these pages. Your decision to use as many of these routines as possible *will* make a difference, a dramatic one if we all join forces.

Motor vehicles are the major polluters of America's air. As car owners, each of us shares some of the blame for the environmental mess we find ourselves in. As a driving population working together, we *can* have a great impact on returning the land and its air to their more pristine natural states. But don't breathe easy for now; the road ahead is still fraught with bad air and pollution potholes.

I was recently in Los Angeles on a business-related driving trip and had the opportunity to spend a few days there. It had been a number of years since I had been in the area, and I immediately noticed that the smog problem had not changed. If anything, it was worse. A couple of days in the damp murkiness was enough for me.

My suspicion was confirmed as I began to drive to Tucson, Arizona, on Interstate 10. Years ago when you drove east of Los

Angeles, you could bet your boots that once you got to the Banning area between San Bernardino and Palm Springs the smog would abate. It was as if someone had put up a wall at the point where the lush vegetation began to turn into high desert and would not permit the smog to go any farther.

Palm Springs, which was just another 20 miles or so from this mythical wall, was always pristine, as was the valley that stretched ahead toward Indio. The contrast was stunning: You could see forever. The San Jacinto Mountains, with Palm Springs snuggled at the base, were always an impressive sight.

But the wall wasn't there this time. The smog bore on, invading the desert canyons and washes. Like a brown blanket, it had moved into the once-inviolable desert. Palm Springs was not visible from the highway anymore. Mt. San Jacinto was like a giant iceberg whose tip was barely visible through a thick fog.

I found it hard to believe that the wall was no more, and that the dirt and pollution covered the desert floor and surrounding mountains all the way to Indio and beyond. Even the tough California antipollution laws had not been enough to stem the onslaught of obnoxious messages that poured from the exhausts of ever-increasing numbers of cars.

I thought to myself, if that can happen in California in just a few short years, it can happen anywhere. And it is happening. But we still have time to do something about it.

California has been the sacrificial lamb; no need for other states to follow suit. We *know* what happens when there are too many cars and not enough emissions controls, when drivers just don't care for their cars, and we will have only ourselves to blame if we let the same thing happen in other cities and states.

Each day when I drive into town from the Tucson Mountains where I live, I cringe when I see what our vehicles are doing. Visible layers of brown smog are now the rule rather than the exception.

What price can we place on pure air and quality of life? Can we be inconvenienced too much? Look around you and envision a day in the not-too-distant future when your favorite vistas won't be visible except for times when the inversion layer is on vacation.

Is that what you want? What your children deserve? If we continue—even at the pace we have now set—that is what we will get. The time is now; the choice is ours. What we do now will be irrevocable proof of how we feel about the planet and the generations who will inherit it.

APPENDIX

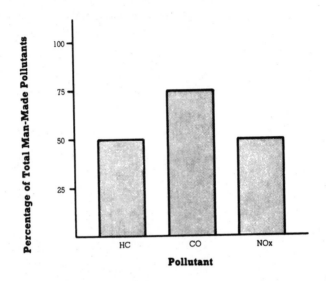

FIGURE 1   The Percentage of Man-made
Pollutants Caused By Automobiles
(*Source: Mitchell International*)

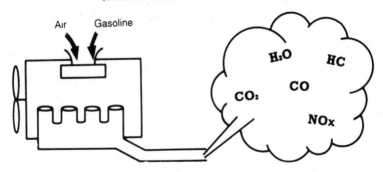

FIGURE 2   By-products of Imperfect Combustion in a Modern
Engine (*Source: Mitchell International*)

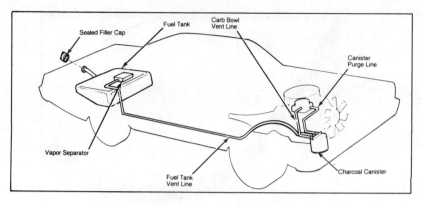

FIGURE 3   **Typical Evaporative Emissions Control System**
(*Source: Mitchell International*)

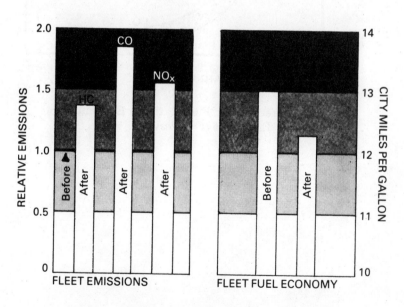

FIGURE 4   **Effects of Private Garage Tampering**
(*Courtesy EPA*)

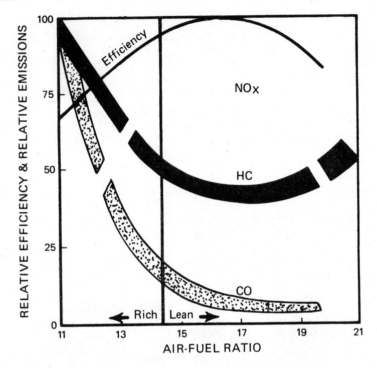

FIGURE 5   **Effect of Air/Fuel Ratio on Efficiency and Emissions** (*Courtesy EPA*)

TABLE 1. **Areas Not Meeting the National Ambient Air Quality Standard (NAAQS) for Ozone Based on 1987–89 Air Quality Data.**

Metropolitan Area

Albany-Schenectady-Troy, NY
Allentown-Bethlehem, PA-NJ
Atlanta, GA
Atlantic City, NJ
Altoona, PA
Bakersfield, CA
Baltimore, MD
Baton Rouge, LA
Beaumont-Port Arthur, TX
Birmingham, AL
Boston, MA
Buffalo, NY
Canton, OH
Charleston, WV
Charlotte-Gastonia-Rock Hill, NC
Chicago, IL-IN-WI
Cincinnati, OH-KY-IN
Cleveland-Akron-Lorain, OH
Columbus, OH
Dallas-Fort Worth, TX
Dayton-Springfield, OH
Detroit-Ann Arbor, MI
Edmonson County, KY
El Paso, TX
Erie, PA
Essex County, NY
Evansville, IN-KY
Fayetteville, NC
Fresno, CA
Grand Rapids, MI
Greenbrier County, WV
Greensboro-Winston Salem-High Point, NC
Greenville-Spartanburg, SC
Hancock County, ME
Harrisburg-Lebanon-Carlisle, PA
Hartford, CT
Houston-Galveston-Brazoria, TX
Huntington-Ashland, WV-KY-OH
Indianapolis, IN
Jefferson County, NY

Johnson City-Kingsport-Bristol, TN-VA
Johnstown, PA
Kansas City, MO-KS
Kewaunee County, WI
Knox County, ME
Knoxville, TN
Lake Charles, LA
Lancaster, PA
Lewiston-Auburn, ME
Lexington-Fayette, KY
Lincoln County, ME
Livingston County, KY
Los Angeles-Anaheim-Riverside, CA
Louisville, KY-IN
Manchester, NH
Memphis, TN-AR-MS
Miami-Ft. Lauderdale, FL
Milwaukee-Racine, WI
Modesto, CA
Montgomery, AL
Muskegon, MI
Nashville, TN
New York, NY-NJ-CT
Norfolk-Virginia Beach-Newport News, VA
Owensboro, KY
Parkerburg-Marietta, WV-OH
Philadelphia, PA-NJ-DE
Pittsburgh, PA
Portland, ME
Portsmouth-Dover-Rochester, NH
Poughkeepsie, NY
Providence, RI-MA
Raleigh-Durham, NC
Reading, PA
Richmond-Petersburg, VA
Sacramento, CA
St. Louis, MO-IL
Salt Lake City-Ogden, UT
San Diego, CA

San Francisco-Oakland-San Jose, CA
Santa Barbara-Santa Maria-Lompoc
Scranton-Wilkes-Barre, PA
Sheboygan, WI
Smyth County, VA
South Bend-Mishawaka, IN
Springfield, MA
Stockton, CA
Sussex County, DE
Tampa-St. Petersburg-Clearwater,
  FL

Toledo, OH
Visalia-Tulare-Porterville, CA
Waldo County, ME
Washington, DC-MD-VA
Worcester, MA
York, PA
Youngstown-Warre, OH (Inc.
  Sharon, PA)

Source: EPA's air quality data system, the Aerometric Information and Re-
trieval System (AIRS), with supplemental data from EPA Regional Offices.

TABLE 2.   **Areas Not Meeting the National Ambient Air
Quality Standard (NAAQS) for Carbon Monoxide Based on
1988–89 Air Quality Data.**

Metropolitan Area

Anchorage, AK
Albuquerque, NM
Baltimore, MD
Boston, MA
Chico, CA
Cleveland, OH
Colorado Springs, CO
Denver-Boulder, CO
Duluth, MN-WI
El Paso, TX
Fairbanks North Star Borough
Fort Collins, CO
Fresno, CA
Greensboro-Winston Salem-High
  Point, NC
Hartford, CT
Josephine County, OR (Grants Pass)
Klamath County, OR (Klamath Falls)
Las Vegas, NV
Los Angeles, CA
Medford, OR

Memphis, TN-AR-MS
Minneapolis-St. Paul, MN-WI
Missoula County, MT
Modesto, CA
New York, NY-NJ-CT
Philadelphia, PA-NJ-DE
Phoenix, AZ
Portland-Vancouver, OR-WA
Provo-Orem, UT
Raleigh-Durham, NC
Reno, NV
Sacramento, CA
San Diego, CA
San Francisco-Oakland-San Jose, CA
Seattle-Tacoma, WA
Spokane, WA
Steubenville-Weirton, OH-WV
Stockton, CA
Syracuse, NY
Washington, DC-MD-VA
Winnebago County, WI (Oshkosh)

Source: EPA's air quality data system, the Aerometric Information and Re-
trieval System (AIRS) with supplemental data from EPA Regional Offices.

RESOURCE GUIDE

American Automobile Association (AAA)
1000 AAA Drive
Heathrow, FL 32746-5063
(407) 444-4000
Performance and recycling tips.

American Lung Association
1740 Broadway
New York, NY 10019
(212) 315-8700
Write for brochures: "Car Care and Clean Air" and "Get a Check-up for Your Car."

American Petroleum Institute (API)
1220 L Street, N.W.
Washington, DC 20005
(202) 682-8000
General information concerning the petroleum industry and its products.

American Public Transit Association
1201 New York Avenue, N.W.
Suite 400
Washington, DC 20005
(202) 898-4000
Brochure: "The Clean-Air Alternative."

Automotive Dismantlers and Recyclers Association
10400 Eaton Place
Suite 203
Fairfax, VA 22030
(703) 385-1001
Consumer recycling brochure.

Automotive Information Council (AIC)
13505 Dulles Technology Drive
Herndon, VA 22071
(703) 904-0700
Bibliographies of EPA publications and articles about alternative fuels, clean air, pollution, recycling, catalytic converters, hazardous waste, and emissions. Additional information about motor oil disposal.

Automotive News
965 East Jefferson
Detroit, MI 48207
(313) 446-6000
Weekly magazine covering all aspects of the automotive industry.

**Automotive Service
Association (ASA)**
1901 Airport Freeway
Bedford, TX 76095
(817) 283-6205
Referrals to other organizations
based on specific needs or questions.

**Clean Air Working Group
(CAWG)**
818 Connecticut Avenue, N.W.
Washington, DC 20006
(202) 857-0370
General information about alternative fuels; referrals to other
organizations for specific problems.

**Consumer Information
Center**
Pueblo, CO 81009
Free copy of the Consumer's Resource Handbook.

**Energy Conservation
Coalition**
1525 New Hampshire Avenue,
N.W.
Washington, DC 20036
(202) 745-4874
Organization that helps to coordinate national energy policy.

**Environmental Protection
Agency (EPA)**
Office of Mobile Sources
401 M Street, S.W.
ANR455901WT
Washington, DC 20460
(202) 382-7647

Pamphlets on nonconforming
cars (overseas purchases), high-
altitude emissions, emissions
test failures, emission control
warranties, and catalytic converters. State offices provide information regarding motor oil
disposal and/or recycling.

Friends of the Earth
218 D Street, S.E.
Washington, DC 20003
(202) 544-2600
General information on environmental issues; educational material for children.

Helm, Inc.
P.O. Box 07130
Detroit, MI 48207
(313) 883-1430: information
(800) 782-4356: Credit Card order
only
Owner's manual source.

The Mileage Co.
P.O. Box 40063
Tucson, AZ 85717
Source for solid lubricants such
as Slick 50 and molybdenum disulfide and the Auto Economizer
filter.

**Motor Vehicle
Manufacturers Association**
7430 Second Avenue
Suite 300
Detroit, MI 48202
(313) 872-4311
Source for general information
concerning cars built by domes-
tic manufacturers.

M.U.S.T. Modern Underhood Systems Technology
published by
Mitchell
Box 26260
San Diego, CA 92126-0260
Contains "Emission Control Training Manual" section.

National Corn Growers Association
World Headquarters
1000 Executive Parkway
St. Louis, MO (314) 275-9915
Information about ethanol ("The Clean Air Fuel") and the progress of Clean Air legislation.

National Energy Education Development (NEED) Project
NEED Headquarters
P.O. Box 2518
Reston, VA 22090
(703) 860-5029
With 32 state offices and 180 regional committees, the NEED project, launched by Congressional Resolution, is the country's foremost energy education network. Integrates energy education activities into the curricular and co-curricular lives of 5,000 member schools and their communities. Helps students of all ages understand the many ways energy is produced and used.

National Highway Traffic Safety Administration (NYTSA)
Department of Transportation
Washington, DC 20690
Auto Safety Hot Line (Recalls)
(800) 424-9393
(202) 366-0123

Renewable Fuels Foundation
201 Massachusetts Avenue, N.W.
Suite C-4
Washington, DC 20002
(800) 542-FUEL
Information for automobile service technicians about alternative fuels and changes in gasoline.

Shell Oil Company
P.O. Box 4681
Houston, TX 77210
Attn: Larry Olejnik
Write for pamphlet "Protect Your Car and the Environment."

Sierra Club
408 C Street, N.E.
Washington, DC 20002
(202) 547-1141
What you can do to reduce global warming: automobile efficiency, lower emissions, and alternative fuels. Information about Clean Cars/Clean Fuels amendments.

The Society of Automotive Engineers (SAE)
400 Commonwealth Drive
Warrendale, PA 15096
(412) 776-4841
Technical books and papers on all aspects of motor vehicles.

The Society of Tribologists and Lubrication Engineers (STLE)
838 Busse Highway
Park Ridge, IL 60068-2376
(708) 825-5536
Technical books and papers on the study of friction, lubrication, and wear in mechanical devices.

Tire Industry Safety Council
National Press Building
Suite 844
Washington, DC 20045
(202) 783-1022

Scrap tire disposal and recycling information. Consumer Tire Guide for care and safety. Scrap tire processors directory.

Uniform Tire Quality Grading System
U.S. Department of Transportation
NHTSA
General Services Division
Room 6117
400 Seventh Street, S.W.
Washington, DC 20590

Worldwatch Institute
1776 Massachusetts Avenue, N.W.
Washington, DC 20036
(202) 452-1999
Write for listing of Worldwatch Paper series.

GLOSSARY

Aldehydes, ketones, carboxylic acids. Partially burned hydrocarbons (HC) that are formed during the combustion process of gasoline and other hydrocarbon fuels.

Carbon dioxide (CO_2). A colorless gas exhaled by animals and needed by all green things for photosynthesis. Also produced when organic or vegetable matter is combusted. A major constituent of car exhaust, it is often implicated as being the major gas responsible for the perceived global warming trend of recent years.

Carbon monoxide (CO). A colorless, odorless and very poisonous gas that is a major constituent of car exhaust especially at engine idle. As little as 0.3 percent by volume can be lethal within 30 minutes.

Chlorofluorocarbons (CFC). More commonly known as freon, escapes from automobile and other air conditioners. CFCs contain fluorine, a poisonous gas that aggressively attacks and depletes the earth's ozone layer.

Evaporative emissions. Emissions formed by the evaporation of gasoline or other automotive fuels.

Exhaust emissions. The tail pipe products of incomplete combustion of gasoline or other fuels.

Grams per mile (gpm). Measurement of exhaust gases used in government cycle emissions tests over an actual road course.

Greenhouse effect. The result of heat trapped on the earth's surface by man-made gases (mainly carbon dioxide), which causes the overall temperature of the earth to rise.

Hydrocarbons (HC). Organic compounds consisting of hydrogen and oxygen molecules. Gasoline is a most common hydrocarbon.

Lead (tetraethyl lead). An extremely toxic additive used in leaded gasoline to increase octane and provide valve wear protection. By law, current available leaded gasolines cannot contain more than 0.1 grams per gallon (gpg) of lead.

Lead oxides, lead halogenides. Compounds formed when leaded gasoline is burned in an engine. Present in the exhaust and as engine deposits.

Miles per gallon (mpg). The average distance a car can travel on one gallon of fuel.

Nitrogen dioxide (NO_2). See nitrous oxides. NO_2 is the main ingredient in the brownish haze we have become accustomed to seeing hanging over our cities.

Nitrous oxides (NOx). Usually a combination of colorless and odorless nitrogen oxide (NO) and toxic, pungent red-brown nitrogen dioxide (NO_2). Nitrous oxides are a major constituent of smog.

Ozone. A form of oxygen with a pungent odor. Formed naturally in the upper atmosphere, its color gives the sky its bluish hue. Ozone forms a protective layer that screens out many of the sun's harmful ultraviolet rays before they reach the earth. It is also a major constituent of photochemical smog.

Paraffins, olefins, aromatic hydrocarbons. Unburned hydrocarbons (HC) that are formed when gasoline and other hydrocarbon fuels are only partially combusted.

Particulate matter. Solids such as carbon and some liquids that are found in exhaust gases.

Parts per million (ppm). A unit of measurement of exhaust gas components. Usually used when the content is too small to be expressed as a percentage.

Photochemical smog. See smog.

Smog. Created when unburned hydrocarbons (HC) and nitrous oxides (NOx) combine in the presence of sunlight. These then react to form ozone, nitrogen dioxide and nitrogen nitrate.

Stoichiometric. The ideal fuel/air ratio, usually 14.7 parts air to one part fuel. Modern computer-controlled cars must maintain a fuel/air ratio as close to stoichiometric as possible in order for the catalytic converter to work at peak efficiency.

Sulfur oxides. Formed when gasoline with sulfur impurities is combusted.

Unburned or partially burned hydrocarbons (HC). Organic compounds such as paraffins, olefins, aromatics, aldehydes, ketones and carboxylic acids that contain hydrogen and carbon in varying amounts. Many hydrocarbons are considered carcinogenic. Unburned hydrocarbons, always present when an internal combustion engine does not operate at 100-percent efficiency, are another main component of photochemical smog.

Volatile organic compounds (VOCs). The unburned hydrocarbon (HC) portions of gasoline.